Asha Alexander

Developing Competencies for Competitiveness in Business Education

D1807263

Asha Alexander

Developing Competencies for Competitiveness in Business Education

Scholar's Press

Impressum / Imprint

Bibliografische Information der Deutschen Nationalbibliothek: Die Deutsche Nationalbibliothek verzeichnet diese Publikation in der Deutschen Nationalbibliografie; detaillierte bibliografische Daten sind im Internet über http://dnb.d-nb.de abrufbar.

Bibliographic information published by the Deutsche Nationalbibliothek: The Deutsche Nationalbibliothek lists this publication in the Deutsche Nationalbibliografie; detailed bibliographic data are available in the Internet at http://dnb.d-nb.de.

Coverbild / Cover image: www.ingimage.com

Verlag / Publisher:
Scholar's Press
ist ein Imprint der / is a trademark of
OmniScriptum GmbH & Co. KG
Heinrich-Böcking-Str. 6-8, 66121 Saarbrücken, Deutschland / Germany
Email: info@scholars-press.com

Herstellung: siehe letzte Seite /
Printed at: see last page
ISBN: 978-3-639-70059-6

Contents

Chapter 1: Overview of Business Education

Chapter 2: Review of Literature

Chapter 3: Research Methodology

Chapter 4: Models and Philosophies of Competencies

Chapter 5: Conceptual Issues Impacting Learning in Business Education

Chapter 6: Assessing Competencies

List of Figures

Preface

Managerial competencies for the business students are most critical for their career growth and development in organizations. To overcome the complex challenges faced by the organizations, increased attention has to be paid to continuous development of managerial competencies to ensure success in business world. There is a growing base of theory and practical activities to support this. The book focuses on overview of business education, literature review covering the challenges faced by business education, research methodology, conceptual issues impacting learning in Business education, Model and philosophies of competencies and assessing the level of attainment of competencies in business students. The book would be of great help to students, academicians, research scholars and professional to develop and assess their managerial competencies.

Acknowledgement

The composition and substance of this paperback have been deeply influenced by business   students. I would like to take this opportunity to first and foremost thank   the   Almighty God for being my strength and guide in the writing of this book.

I wish to thank My Husband, My son, My parents, My sister and all my family members for always being there for me . I am obliged to my friend Ms Jennifer Rocio Camargo who has helped me in formatting my work. I am grateful to Business Administration Department, Jubail University College and Royal Commission of Jubail, for the encouraging the publication of all my research work. I would also like to thank   Dr Ghadah Al Saleh our college deputy for always being supportive to me .I am privileged to express my heartfelt thanks to my great friend, Dr. Nailah Ayub for her guidance in data analysis. I am also indebted to large number of authors whose work I cite throughout the text, without their efforts I could not have written this book. I would like to acknowledge the contribution of all the students of business education for their valuable response to the questionnaire carried out for the study.

Last but not the least I wish to say 'Thank you' to everyone at Scholars' press publishing house for this book to happen.

Asha Alexander

Chapter 1

OVERVIEW OF BUSINESS EDUCATION

Introduction

With the progression of globalization, the prospect for the skilled and competent has grown remarkably and business education in world is mushrooming at a rapid pace. Some of the well commended business personalities of the world have graduated from the best management schools in world. This is an acknowledgment to the outstanding learning offered at these institutes. Women too have made up advancement worldwide of practising business management (Jennifer Lewington ; 2013,Widget Finn ;2012).This drive has been gaining by leaps and bounds even in Saudi Arabia .The Kingdom having strict Islamic values has brought with it increasing opportunities for women in both education and employment . One of the main objectives of business education is to contribute to the development and prosperity of Saudi society while observing the principles of Islam. The objective behind pursuing business education is that formal training will offer a more efficient and effective means of acquiring the necessary competencies required to enact managerial roles. (Pfeffer & Fong, 2002).

1

History of Management Education

At the beginning of the 20th century business became more composite. Conglomerates grew in size and complexity to cope with the challenges created through industrialization. The growing size of these conglomerates created a need for individuals who were capable of successfully managing them. In previous decades due to absence of business education managers came from a variety of backgrounds including economics and the legal professions. But some universities in the United States of America saw this as an opportunity and introduced new education named as Master of Business Administration .The objective was to provide potential managers with curriculum which would familiarize them with the tasks and challenges they would face in the new corporations. Figure 1.1 shows the chronology of business education.

By World War Two, many managers in USA enterprises had gone to business schools and as a result many American companies were considered to be very successful both within the home market, and around the world. The same trends that drove the development of business schools in the Americas came to Europe. The business schools in France and United Kingdom began in the 1950's. There were significant differences between schools in USA and Europe (Peter, K 2006). Europe considered the diverse and international nature of business, they were also influenced by the business education in USA. These European schools developed a variety of models which were suited to the particular nature of business in that country, or an internationally oriented philosophy which sought to address the needs of international business (Allan, P.O, 2010). In general the curriculum of business schools provided a simulation of the concerns faced by managers in academically rigorous surroundings.

2

1857	The Budapest Business School was founded in the Austrian Empire. It was the first business school in Central Europe.
1868	The Ca' Foscari University the oldest business school in Italy was founded in Venice.
1871	The Rouen Business School the second oldest French business school was established. It is now known as the NEOMA Business School.
1881	The Wharton School of the University of Pennsylvania was the first business school in the United States'
1898	The University of St. Gallen established the first university in Switzerland teaching business and economics.
1900	The Tuck School of Business at Dartmouth College, was founded in the Unites States. It conferred the first advanced degree in business, A Master of Science in Commercial Sciences, the predecessor to the MBA.
1902	The Birmingham Business School was the first business school in the United Kingdom.
1906	The McGill School of Commerce was founded as part of McGill University in Montreal, Canada, eventually known as Desautels Faculty of Management.
1906	The Warsaw School of Economics (SGH) was established as the first university in Poland dedicated to teaching commerce and economics.
1908	Harvard Business School was founded at Harvard University It's the first program in the world to offer the Master of Business Administration degree.

1909	The oldest business school, Stockholm School of Economics was founded on the initiative of the Swedish business sector. Hanken School of Economics was also established in the same year in Helsinki, Finland.
1936	The Norwegian School of Economics, the oldest business school in Norway was established.
1946	The Thunderbird School of Global Management, now known as the American Institute for Foreign Trade, was the first graduate management school established which focused exclusively on global business.
1949	The University of Pretoria in South Africa founded this oldest business school in Africa.
1949	XLRI - India's oldest business management school was founded.
1953	IISWBM was the first institute in India to offer an MBA degree.
1954	The Faculty of Management Studies (FMS), University of Delhi was among one of the oldest and reputed business schools in India.
1955	The Institute of Business Administration, Karachi was the first business school in Pakistan to be established outside North America to offer an MBA degree.
1991	The IEDC-B led School of Management in the Eastern Europe was the first business school to offer an MBA program.
1994	CEIBS (China Europe International Business School) in China was the first business school to have received funding from the European Commission.

Figure 1.1 Chronology of Business Education (http://en.wikipedia.org/wiki/Business_school)

4

This twofold requirement indicates that schools should combine a structured, analytical approach to business with the parallel focus on getting things done. Within this set of common goals, a wide degree of diversity exists between the different business schools. There are different philosophies on how the curriculum should be based; on how long the overall education should be; on what types of industries and what geographic areas the education focuses on (Rubin and Dierdorff, 2009).The business   education has a powerful reputation still it cannot change the individual completely but it is a broadening process which develops management ability in individuals who have the potential for management.

A business education is a university-level institution that confers degrees in business administration or management. Such a school can also be known as a business college, college of business, college of business administration, school of business or b-school. A business school teaches topics such as accounting, administration, strategy, economics, entrepreneurship, finance, human resource management, information systems, logistics, marketing, organizational psychology, organizational behavior, public relations, research methods and real estate among others. Several business schools focus their teaching in the order of the use of case studies.

Business education is understood broadly to encompass education and development for managers. This includes not only MBAs, postgraduate coursework, executive education activities, but also undergraduate programs and various outreach, collaborative and business engagement activities (ABDC;2012).In North America, business schools are business school are normally considered as university education that recommends a graduate Master of Business Administration degrees and/or undergraduate bachelor's degrees. In Europe, key business schools are owned by the Chambers of Commerce including ESCP Europe, founded in 1819 (ESCP; 2013) .

Common degrees offered by many universities are as follows are as follows.

- Bachelor's Degrees: BBA (Bachelor of Business Administration), BBus (Bachelor of Business) and BBusSc (Bachelor of Business Science)
- Master's Degrees: MBA (Master of Business Administration), MBM, (Master of Management). At Oxford and Cambridge business schools an MPhil or MSc, is awarded in place of an MA.
- Doctoral Degrees: PhD in Management or Business Doctorate (Doctor of Philosophy), Doctor of Professional Studies (DPS)

At present there are three main accreditation body for business schools in the United States; namely The Association to Advance Collegiate Schools of Business (AACSB)and The Accreditation Council for Business Schools & Programs (ACBSP) (AACSB,2006) and The International Assembly for Collegiate Business Education (IACBE) (ACBSP, 2010). In Europe, the regional accreditation association is The European Foundation for Management Development (EFMD). Every year, renowned business publications such as The Economist, Eduniversal, U.S. News & World Report, Fortune, Financial Times, Business Week and The Wall Street Journal publish rankings of selected MBA educations and business schools. The academic research is considered to be an important feature and popular way to gauge the prestige of business schools.

The Graduate Management Admission Test (GMAT) is a registered trademark of the Graduate Management Admission Council. More than 5,900 educations offered by more than 2,100 universities and institutions use the GMAT exam as part of the selection criteria for their educations. Business education use the test as a criterion for admission into a wide range of graduate management educations, including MBA, Master of Accountancy and Master of Finance educations. The GMAT exam is administered in standardized test centers in 112 countries around the world. According to the test owning company, the Graduate Management Admission Council (GMAC,2013) the GMAT assesses analytical writing and problem-solving abilities, while also addressing data sufficiency, logic and critical reasoning skills that it believes to be the vital to the real world.

Women in Management Education

Schools have an imperative role to play in generating extraordinary women leaders like Terry Sullivan, Lorna Donatone, Valerie Jarrett and Sheryl Sandberg. The presence of women in business itself is widely transformational. This diversity will have an astounding impact on the culture of the organization. The growth rate in women taking the GMAT is rapid than men. Figure 1.2 shows the GMAT's total score on the basis of gender and testing year. In the past 10 years, the average growth rate for men was -0.06% while that for women was +1.72. The larger representation of women in classrooms, learning teams and project groups

Gender	2003-04	2004-05	2005-06	2006-07	2007-08	2008-09	2009-10	2010-11	2011-12	2012-13
Men: Number	124,502	120,185	123,811	132,665	149,511	160,733	158,079	151,392	163,686	137,020
Mean Total Score	541	541	548	552	554	552	555	554	557	555
% of year	60.2%	59.9%	60.5%	60.6%	60.5%	60.5%	59.9%	58.6%	57.1%	57.5%
Women: Number	78,679	76,980	79,661	86,412	97,446	104,880	105,900	106,800	122,843	101,336
Mean Total Score	501	500	508	514	518	519	526	530	536	534
% of year	38.0%	38.4%	39.0%	39.4%	39.5%	39.5%	40.1%	41.4%	42.9%	42.5%
No Response: Number	3,671	3,338	1,037	0	0	0	0	0	0	0
Mean Total Score	535	542	547	–	–	–	–	–	–	–
% of year	1.8%	1.7%	0.5%	–	–	–	–	–	–	–
Total: Number	206,852	200,503	204,509	219,077	246,957	265,613	263,979	258,192	286,529	238,356
Mean Total Score	526	525	533	537	540	539	544	544	548	546

Figure 1.2 GMAT: Total Score Means by Gender and Testing Year

gives higher levels of satisfaction with the learning experience among both. Faculty describes better classroom and team results while the corporate recruiters report greater contentment with the talent pool they come across. The more women in business, the greater their impact on productivity. Actions to support and increase the pool of qualified applicants should incorporate:

- Improving K-12 education to promote entry into undergraduate educations.
- Intensify outreach from graduate business schools to undergraduate students.
- Expand public and private financial aid for women students.
- Promote educations like short certificate educations and one-year "Masters in Management" that help undergraduate women transition into business careers.
- Relax H1-B visa requirements for international women seeking to work in the U.S. upon graduation from MBA educations.

The Challenge in Business Education

The 20-year GMAT volume time-series shows growth in tests taken by women. This volume does not directly translate to B-school application since GMAT-takers today have many options beyond the MBA degree. Thus we can infer that more women are applying to B- schools now than 20 years ago.

The following challenges were framed as a 90-minute discussion among the Deans of business schools at Harvard, Virginia (Darden), Northwestern

(Kellogg), Michigan (Ross), Cornell (Johnson), Texas (McCombs), NYU (Stern), Berkeley (Haas), UCLA (Anderson), UNC (Kenan-Flagler), Emory (Goizueta), Carnegie Mellon (Tepper), and Yale (Darden, 2014).

- Business school lifecycle: The profile of a business school student includes 5 years of post-college professional experience and would like to get enough years of post-MBA experience before having children. This issue not only raises challenges for female students but also for men who are increasingly likely to be active co-parents. Re-entry after child-bearing requires mentoring to handle anxiety and build confidence .Thus mentoring has become challenge for business schools to prepare and help alumnae to re-enter the workforce and to retain the female talent.

- Pay gaps and career success: The pay gap between men and women with MBA degrees requires more transparency and research. Women and men negotiate differently for pay. The issue of negotiation must be broadened to include advocacy, self-promotion and career advancement.

- Culture: Research has found that women are less likely to re-frame ethical dilemmas to their advantage and instead see them as ethical issues. They also find that women associate business with immorality more than men do. There is need for training on ethics to have a broader perspective and outlook in the area.

- Leadership: The effective leadership behaviors and the stages of leadership development   are not gender-specific. Women and men may practice leadership in different ways. So there is a need to consider what leaders need in coaching and development.

- Curriculum: The curriculum has to be designed and adapted to reflect the modern workforce and workplace challenges. In the entire field, there remains a relatively small percentage of case studies that feature women .Therefore there is a need for significant changes in the curriculum incorporating these features.
- Social class: The biggest diversity problem is not the difference of genders, but social class. MBA educations draw mainly from the upper middle class rather than from the bottom quartile of the economic scale.
- Undergraduate business education is the biggest major in USA ., occupying about 50% women. MBA educations comprises about 33% women students while the pre-experience master's educations are about 50%. Part-time and EMBA educations are seeing the entry of very talented women into the professional path.

Business Education in Saudi Arabia

In this increasingly globalizing environment, development of Saudi manpower capabilities are regarded as vital factors within the framework of industrial development and the competitiveness of Saudi industry for the future (SIDF, 2013). Figure 1.3 shows Global Competitiveness Index for the Kingdom of Saudi Arabia. It is ranked 24th among the 144 countries in the Global Competitiveness Report 2014-2015. The position makes the Kingdom second highest rated of the 20 largest emerging market economies (WEF, 2014). Figure 1.4 shows the indicator 5th pillar: Higher education and training. It has a strong competitiveness position in the Arab region(AWCR;2013).

The country has seen a number of improvements to its competitiveness in recent years, which have resulted in enhancing the country's educational system by introducing new education programs, research and development initiatives and building numerous schools and universities. Since 1930's, education has benefited from continual private and public support in Saudi Arabia. Figure 1.5 shows the supplementary indicators: perceptions of well being. The Kingdom represents the largest market for education services in the Gulf Cooperation Council (GCC) region, and accounts for 75 percent of total students in the GCC general education (K-12) system (USSABC, 2009).

According to the data released by the ministry of civil services there are more than hundreds of job titles in the field of management. The information from the website of Saudi Arabian Monetary Agency (the central bank) reveals that the number of working Saudi women in the private sector witnessed a huge increase of 85% in 2013 rising to 398,538 from 100,000 in 2011. These huge increases in employment have far outstripped the steady growth of women working in the public sector. The year 2014, witnessed for the first time in the recent history more Saudi women working in the private rather than the public sector. Even though comparatively broad-based, the biggest increase in female employment has been in the retail sector, private teaching and nursing and construction. The rise in the prospect of employment in retail sector is due to government measures of employing only the women in lingerie stores. The construction sector back office, which was once dominated by

Global Competitiveness Index		
GCI 2014–2015	24	5.1
GCI 2013–2014 (out of 148)	20	5.1
GCI 2012–2013 (out of 144)	18	5.2
GCI 2011–2012 (out of 142)	17	5.2
Basic requirements (42.9%)	15	5.7
Institutions	25	5.0
Infrastructure	30	5.2
Macroeconomic environment	4	6.7
Health and primary education	50	6.0
Efficiency enhancers (47.8%)	33	4.6
Higher education and training	57	4.6
Goods market efficiency	35	4.7
Labor market efficiency	64	4.2
Financial market development	30	4.7
Technological readiness	45	4.5
Market size	20	5.1
Innovation and sophistication factors (9.3%)	32	4.2
Business sophistication	30	4.6
Innovation	33	3.8

Figure 1.3 Global Competitiveness Index 2014-2015

13

5th pillar: Higher education and training		
5.01 Secondary education enrollment, gross %*	116.2	7
5.02 Tertiary education enrollment, gross %*	50.9	55
5.03 Quality of the education system	4.1	47
5.04 Quality of math and science education	4.1	73
5.05 Quality of management schools	4.2	78
5.06 Internet access in schools	4.6	63
5.07 Availability of research and training services	4.1	73
5.08 Extent of staff training	4.1	60

Figure 1.4 5th pillar: Higher Education and Training 2014-2015

14

Supplementary indicators: perceptions of well being

	Perception of well being							Perception about community			Perception about government		
	Education quality	Health care quality	Standard of living	Job	Safety	Freedom of choice	Overall life satisfaction on index	Local labor market	Trust in other people	Community	Effort to deal with poor	Actions to preserve the environment	Trust in national government
	% Satisfied				% answering yes	% Satisfied	Least satisfied to most satisfied	% answering good	% answering can be trusted	% answering yes	% Satisfied		% answering yes
	2012	2006-2012	2007-2013	2007-2012	2007-2012	2007-2012	2007-2012	2007-2012	2007-2012	2007-2012	2007-2012	2007-2012	2007-2012
	65	56	77	90	77	59	65	73	36	93	90	56	-

Figure 1.5 Supplementary Indicators: Perceptions of Well Being

expatriate men is also now   replaced by Saudi women. The demand for the labor force in the Kingdom is shown in Figure 1.6.

Conversely, it is worth noting that the number of working Saudi women (both in the public and private sectors) remains comparatively low, at about 831,000, compared with 1.78m Saudi men (and 8.1m expatriates males) despite the fact that women's education levels are now on a par with men, and improving rapidly. The announcement of female business-process outsourcing centre at Riyadh, creating 3,000 jobs is among the recent notable landmarks of 2013. The latest employment data reinforces that the government will seek to boost the number of Saudi workers in the private sector and replacing foreign workers with Saudi female's employees. The government has announced a succession of plans since 2000 for 'Saudi zing' the economy. So there will be a huge demand for workforce and employment opportunities in field of management.

The upward trend of budgetary allocations highlights the Saudi Government's conviction that education is the cornerstone of sustained economic development, as it enhances human capital and knowledge, both essential ingredients for economic growth and social cohesion. Public spending for education is estimated at 5.7 % of the country's Gross Domestic Product (GDP), comparable with UK (5.3 %), Germany (4.3 %) and South Korea (4.2%).Saudi Arabia is ranked first among the Middle Eastern countries in terms of the number of students studying in USA. The plan aims to reduce the number of foreign workers who are currently employed in technical and vocational professions in Saudi Arabia. The priority given to education is evident from the sharp rise in the number of students at all levels from about 547000 in 1970 to over 5 million in 2002. (Human Development Report, 2011).

	2010	2011	2012	2013
Government sector				
Saudis	959,833	998,138	1,089,501	1,224,821
Male	884,715	919,108	1,013,652	1,150,828
Female	589,627	616,748	643,212	718,383
Non-Saudis	295,088	302,360	369,840	432,445
Male	75,118	79,030	76,449	73,993
female	33,677	37,128	36,663	36,203
	41,441	41,902	39,786	37,790
Private sector				
Saudis	6,991,200	7,781,496	8,487,533	9,679,635
Male	724,655	844,476	1,134,633	1,466,853
Female	669,037	744,990	918,793	1,068,315
Non-Saudis	55,618	99,486	215,840	398,538
Male	6,266,545	6,937,020	7,352,900	8,212,782
Female	6,178,130	6,823,554	7,244,206	8,051,394
	88,415	113,466	108,694	161,388

Source: Saudi Arabian Monetary Agency.

Figure 1.6 Labor force in Saudi Arabia

Women Education in Saudi Arabia

According to the World Bank, gross enrollment rate for female was found to be 36.1 percent, of the total gross enrollment rate which was 30.2 percent in 2006.The contribution of women in the field of education is rising which is proved by the fact that there are thousands of female professors throughout the Kingdom (World Bank, 2007). Ms Fayez became the first woman minister deputy education minister in charge of a new department for female students around 2009 (Borger, Julian 2009). In addition, Kingdom provides female students with one of the world's largest scholarship educations and thousands of them have earned doctorates from Western universities. Princess Nora bint Abdul Rahman University (PNU) is the first Women university in Saudi Arabia and largest women-only university in the world. The development of the Kingdom has brought with it increasing opportunities for women in both education and employment. In 1960, the Government undertook the introduction of a national education for girls. By the mid-1970s, about half of Saudi Arabian girls were attending school. Five years later, education was available to all Saudi girls. By 1980, there were six universities for women (MOHE, 2010). Figure 1.7 shows the GMAT score gender wise for the Kingdom.

Citizenship	Gender	2008-9	2009-10	2010-11	2011-12	2012-13
Saudi Arabia	MEN	975	1,201	1,541	1,910	1,745
	WOMEN	224	323	477	753	630
	TOTAL NUMBER	1,199	1,524	2,018	2,663	2,375
	MEAN TOTAL SCORES	353	355	330	301	311

Figure 1.7 GMAT: Total Scores Means By Citizenship, Gender and Testing Year

Currently, more than 300 higher education colleges exist for women in the country alongside universities, and women represent more than 56.6% of the total number of Saudi university students and more than 20% of those benefiting from overseas scholarship education. The percentage is expected to increase in the coming years with the establishment of a number of new universities in major cities in the Kingdom. Saudi women have dazzled international observers by becoming pioneers in a variety of fields, most prominently science and research and by receiving international awards and earning patents. These achievements have been reflected in international reports and statistics. The 2009 Global Education Digest of UNESCO showed that Saudi women come remarkably ahead of western women in terms of obtaining academic degrees (MOHE, 2010). Also the 2009 global gender gap report ranked Saudi Arabia at 25th among countries in terms of the gap between the genders in university registration. The country thus ranked ahead of USA and Germany. As a part of the objectives of the Kingdom's development plans, women in Saudi Arabia today are vigorously pursuing higher education and professional careers and seeking to become active members of society, where their roles are defined in terms of what they can offer for their countries economic, as well as social and cultural development.

The glint of career growth and the revenues earned is drawing the attention of numerous young Saudi female students to the university colleges. Data on the economic status of women in Saudi Arabia are inconsistent, but they suggest substantial economic involvement in the country. (Asha and Areej ,2013). The future economic climate would be characterized by more openness, high competitiveness, new economic trends, information and technology innovations and various numerous challenges in Human resource management (SIDF, 2013). The management education provides the budding managers with the most effective methods of leveraging and managing people in changing environment.

Chapter 2

LITERATURE REVIEW

Relevancy of Business Education

During the last few years, lot of studies about business education has flourished. The recent debate about the value and meaning of management education programs and more generally, the ability of business schools to provide effective business education, put these programs under the spotlight. The scholars from all over the world have tried to disentangle the reasons of their decreasing popularity: Firstly from the nature and quantity of learning actually taking place in such programs, to their impact on salaries and careers. Secondly from the scientific foundation and quality of the knowledge these courses teach, to the kind of skills and competencies students develop .Thirdly from the capacity of the business education programs to evolve and innovate as economy and society change, to the ethical issues involved in teaching business. One critical aspect of management education is the relevance to business graduates as they wonder if business education is really worth to manage in complex environments. (Augier and Teece, 2005; Armstrong, 2005; Connolly, 2003; Mintzberg, 2004; Pfeffer and Fong, 2002, 2003, 2004)

Due to the steady growth and apparent economic prosperity of business schools, the programs are being met with escalating criticism regarding the capabilities they claim to impart. Although such criticisms reach as far back as the dawning of the American business education, this recent round has sparked considerable attention in both the academic and popular press.. More recently, a number of scholars have strongly urged business schools to seriously reconsider their current approach to management education (Bennis & O'Toole, 2005; Ghoshal, 2005; Khurana, 2007; Mintzberg, 2004; Pfeffer & Fong, 2002). The criticisms raised in these recent commentaries span a variety of concerns. For instance, in his highly critical book "Managers, Not management" Mintzberg (2004) argues that management is a professional trade, a craft to be honed through practice and experience, not in the traditional classroom. He further purports that today's conventional management programs are more akin to specialized training grounds for the specific functions of business rather than the broad practice of management.

Misalignment between the Skills Acquired and Required

Pfeffer and Fong (2002) points out substantial misalignment between the mastery of skills acquired in the business education and the impact of real world on those skills. These authors cite studies suggesting that while many business graduates earn considerably more than their non- business counterparts, the effect of this difference is primarily due to pedigree at top programs rather than to the degree itself. Further, they ponts to the fact that till to date, little evidence exists supporting the actual connection between mastery of the management curriculum and subsequent on-the-job behavior. Bennis and O'Toole (2005) strongly proclaim that "business schools have lost their way" by refusing to view management as a profession rather than a science. These authors further deride business schools for enacting this view by hiring and rewarding professors for their research prowess rather than their management experience. As a result, Bennis and O'Toole further argues, that "the focus of graduate business education has become increasingly circumscribed—and less and less relevant to practitioners".

The recent critics assert that the business education is altogether out-of-touch with the "real world" and the requirements of the managers. More specifically, these criticisms appear to converge fairly without a doubt on a single critical issue dealing with the significance of business education. Indeed, referendums for relevancy in business education are said to be moving some areas of the field, such as behavioral science, toward a clear "legitimacy crisis". This crisis has resulted in a dysfunctional and entirely reactive approach to management education including easier coursework, an exclusive focus on current events, grade inflation, an increase in unqualified instructors and reactive curricular decision making. Anecdotally, even casual observers of business education are likely to verify such trends. Yet, for questions of relevancy to have tangible value they must be couched in terms of relevancy to a particular criterion. From this perspective, the answer to whether business education are relevant will drastically differ depending on the criteria used to gauge such relevancy. In light of the various criteria that can be used to assess relevancy, a careful examination of recent criticism reveals a substantial lack of consensus regarding what is actually irrelevant or relevant about contemporary business education. To be sure, passionate arguments regarding relevancy have certainly been proffered on all sides of the debate. However, the sources used to bolster much of this debate often offer equivocal and even contradictory conclusions (Rynes & Trank, 1999).

Recruiters Expectation

Corporate recruiters routinely assert that MBA programs could be more relevant by doing more to inculcate "soft skills" for instance leadership, team player, communication, decision making and interpersonal skills (Eberhardt, McGee, & Moser, 1997). Thus, recruiters place significant value upon the acquisition of people focused managerial capabilities. However, recruiters' actions deliver a different message as they tend to make selection decisions based on the possession of technical skills. Research also shows that students increasingly harbor negative attitudes toward learning such soft skills (Rynes et al., 2003). The business students purport that MBA programs could be more relevant by disposing of anything that is not perceived as "useful" in gaining employment. Even academics themselves add to the lack of consensus regarding relevancy, with some articulating enhanced relevancy through increased behavioral science or evidence-based curricula (Rynes & Trank, 1999), while others argue for a significant departure from the science-based curriculum approach (Bennis & O'Toole, 2005).

Researchers and practitioners alike have raised the issue of the misalignment between the competencies which the MBA curriculum attempts to impart and the competencies which the managers need while on job (Anwar, Al-Shami, & Ahmed, 2006; Blass & Weight, 2005; Elliott & Goodwin, 1994; Gupta, Saunders, & Smith, 2007; Kleiman & Kass, 2007; Rubin & Dierdorff, 2009). While issues like the need to include new and integrative courses have been raised along with curriculum innovation (Navarro, 2008), program design and pedagogical changes too have attracted the attention of critics (Buchowicz & Buchanan, 2008; Dumas, Blodgett, Carlson, Pant, & Venkatraman, 2000).

Growing importance on Economic Incentive

In contemporary work organizations, managerial capabilities have typically been acquired through informal work experiences. Research studies have shown that 70–90% of workplace learning occurs through on-the-job experiences, informal training and mentoring (Tannenbaum, 1997). While trial and error and informal experiences can be rich source for learning to perform the managerial role, they are rather inefficient settings that are extraordinarily unsystematic .As economic incentives are linked to formal training the person's willinging to gain important managerial capabilities frequently turn to formal training opportunities such as certificate programs, university degree programs, or university-based executive education (Arnaldo etal 2009). At this point, the prevailing logic is that formal training will put forward a more efficient and effective means of attaining the essential competencies required to perform managerial roles. The customary adoption of this logic is evidently visible and witnessed in the growth of graduate schools of business, where over 100,000 graduate degrees in business were awarded annually (Pfeffer & Fong, 2002).

Criterion for Assessment

There arises a need to move further beyond the uncertainty that surround the concerns of relevancy in business education by setting up more productive criterion and systematic investigation .The most basic element of any learning context; that is to say, the contemporary content delivered in MBA programs can be one such criterion by which the relevancy of business education can be assessed. This criterion allows for a more systematic and generalizable assessment of relevancy and helps to investigate the extent to which trained content aligns with the work that is requisite to "real-life" managerial roles.

To assess MBA relevancy as a training ground for managerial work, there is a need to necessitate priori understanding of the nature of topical managerial work and its allied requirements (Rubin etal 2009)

Innovative Ways of Teaching Management

Educating include business professors enacting their teaching and researching perceived roles influenced by their professional identities (Greenberg et al., 2007). This pedagogical conceptions on management education role can further be understood in an integrated way by mapping academics' working life activities disseminated among domains namely teaching, learning research and administrative through the temporal landscape perspective .The management research has its roots in positivist epistemology (Johnson & Duberley, 2000). There curriculum is based on Cartesian scholastic education and discipline. A "banking model of education" has been developed in Brazilian business schools transforming them into "managers maker factories" that is still flourishing .In Brazil few business school scholars are endorsing innovative ways of teaching management by using arts , literature and drama to develop students' managerial competencies (Villardi etal 2013) .The underlying belief is that experiential learning and a dialogical process of teaching-learning provide students with a transformative learning experience (Cranston; 2006). Here the role of education is to facilitate the student self-knowledge and their active participation in the social context. In performing such a role the use of pedagogy is to recognize as an education science application which builds up a teaching-learning relationship (Villardi etal 2013).

Ethics and Human-Centered Curriculum in Business Education

There are sharp criticisms on the role played by business education graduates in corporate scandals and the alleged lack of courses that develop the powers of critical thinking and moral reasoning (Podolny, 2009). So the business schools have introduced changes to the curriculum to a smaller extent, like the inclusion of courses on Ethics as a compulsory requirement. This will help the future managers to understand and value their ethical responsibilities to society (Evans, Treviño, & Weaver, 2006; Swanson, 2004).

Authors have also argued for a shift in favor of Human-Centered Curriculum in business education (Giacalone & Thompson, 2006). In a current study, Bell et al. (2009) cite moral, ethical, and business reasons for mandatory diversity education so that the management students are well-equipped to participate in diverse situations. Researchers have suggested that the curriculum "must be inculcated with ethical questions and analyses reflecting the complex challenges business leaders face" (Bennis & O'Toole, 2005).

Business education, suffers from a lack of general culture, scientific and humanities knowledge and a critical spirit. Therefore, it is recommended to rescue business education by creating an awareness of the consequences of what is taught, focusing on the symbolic world and its role in organizations, considering the "whole" relational meaning of every human fact, creating a taste for reading, reflection and intellectual effort and reflecting the meaning of the critical spirit and humility(Villardi etal 2003).

Identification of the problem

The Books like "What They Don't Teach You at B- School" talk about the most important requirements of managers such as success, intuition, courage and common sense which are not guarantee by management program. The B-Schools may teach analysis but real life needs more synthesis and it's the workplace that proves to be a better teacher. B-Schools can make managers but not leaders as these leadership qualities have to be developed. (Meenakshi Radhakrishnan-Swami, 2007).The schools need to concentrate on the art of management. Besides this in recent years, against a backdrop of corporate scandals and a difficult economy, schools of business has ensued about the value of management programs from multiple stakeholder perspectives with an eye toward improving the overall quality of graduate management education .The MBA curricula should be erected, suggesting a skewed emphasis on economic theory, stakeholders and financial management.

The present study is based on a recent study by Dierdorff et al. (Dierdorff, Rubin, & Morgeson, 2009) and Rubin and Dierdorff (2009). Though Dierdorff et al. (2009) depended on an empirically derived competency model from 8,633 present managers crosswise 52 managerial occupations to arrive at a set of required managerial competencies.Rubin and Dierdorff (2009) studied the relevancy of the MBA curricula in relation to managerial competency requisites across 373 schools. The most significant managerial competencies were found to be the very competencies least represented in MBA curricula. Hence there exist a mismatch between curriculum and competencies. Other concerns that have been addressed are having more domain-specific curricular areas including the need for reinforcing technology management, innovation and entrepreneurship, research methodology, systems thinking, cultural diversity and competence, behavioral science and ethics. So there is the urgent need to review the sustainability and viability of the existing business education by focusing on managerial competencies for different roles in global organisations.

All in all, there is enough discussion both by researchers and practitioners regarding the relevancy of business school curricula and its alignments with managerial competencies needed on the job. On the basis of given literature review there exist a gap in the study of developing managerial competencies for female university college students in Saudi Arabia. The actual detailed studies on this topic are scarce, the only studies that were carried out was the analysis of the management competency in university female students in eastern province of Saudi Arabia (Asha and Farah, 2013).The focus of the present study was to widen the scope of study with respect to developing and assessing competencies for competiveness in business education.

Chapter 3

RESEARCH METHODOLOGY

Overview

Competency based business education proposes to guide the professional development of students by emphasizing on the core competencies required to be effective managers. There is a need to help students develop these skills and knowledge that will be required to be successful in today's global context.

According to the editors at the wall street journal the recruiters look for communication, inter personal skills, team work, personal ethics, leadership and strategic thinking when hiring college graduates. Extensive research shows that these managerial competencies are needed even in technical jobs among professional staff members and line managers. The Business programs accreditation bodies have also laid down in their eligibility procedures developing competencies in the area of communication, ethical understanding, reasoning abilities, analytical skills, multicultural and diversity training, reflective thinking skills, ethical and legal responsibilities in organizations and society. In competency based learning the focus is on how real world managers can use these general competencies as they address the daily challenges of managing and leading their organizations which results into active student learning.

Competency based learning system are intended for use in introductory management classes taught at any level in the university. It introduces the core managerial competencies that are examined throughout this course and includes a self assessment inventory that students can use to measure their current standing on the core managerial competencies. After scoring their self assessment inventory students will gain insight into their current areas of strength and thus altering areas which requires improvement. With their heightened self awareness, students will find it easy to connect personally with the relevant material.

Title of the Study

Developing Competencies for competitiveness in Business Education

Objective of the Study

In light of the domain for research, the study was undertaken:

- To determine the current level of student's attainment in the core managerial competencies.
- To analyze the impact of Academic year on core managerial competencies
- To analyze the impact of core managerial competencies on assessments of students
- To determine the achievement of the students learning outcomes using rubrics

Research Design

A research design is a framework or blue print for conducting the research project. It provides details of the procedure necessary for obtaining the information needed to structure and solve research problem. A research design lays the foundation for conducting the research project. The cross-sectional descriptive research design was used for conducting this research work .This design enables the researcher to study the problem at given point of time, of the population of interest. Primary and secondary data has been used in order to identify the research problem, develop an approach for it and to formulate an appropriate research design.

Universe of study

The universe of study consists of female business education students of University College in the Eastern province of Kingdom of Saudi Arabia. Since the number of female students in business education is quite big and as the study is being undertaken by an individual researcher, it was beyond the capacity of individual researcher to pursue the study on hundred percent enumerative bases. Hence the study has been carried out using adequate sample size containing female business education students of University College.

Sampling Design

The sample is selected considering the following factors:

a. The data for the entire period of study from the year 2011 is available. The business education program should have the duration of four academic years, plus one academic year for the preparatory program. The four years spent as an undergraduate at a university college are typically known as the freshman, sophomore, junior and senior.

 b. Business education program should focus on developing managerial competencies among the students. To foster excellence, the concerns of managers are merged with managerial competencies. To appreciate the role of today's managers and in years ahead a focus on understanding of the core managerial competencies is a must. Competencies based learning makes use of study material, practice activities and feedback directed at helping the students learn these competencies. Students benefit by having the competencies defined and clarified to foster early success in their careers.

c. The process of guided learning should include the following:

- Throughout the learning, students are exposed with examples of managerial competencies in action so that they can assess their competencies and begin to develop their potential as effective managers and leaders.
- Every section of competency based learning should define the learning goals which form the basis of 'easy to use' integrated learning system.
- Every session should opens with a current, real world account, stimulate discussions and encourage reflective thinking. This will promote competency development by providing opportunities to apply and analyze important chapter concepts and related competencies.
- Learning should encourage students to venture into cyberspace to discover additional information to engage in their own personal development.
- Experiential exercises should be carried out which include activities for small group discussion, personal planning activities and knowledge quizzes. It will stimulate students to delve deeply into chapter's concept and also provides feedback to student regarding their emotional intelligence , reaction to change , cultural values and so on by self assessment questionnaire.
- Substantive case study should be used that challenges to apply chapter concepts to an actual situation. Focused discussions questions at the end of each case would help students to analyze evaluate and suggest courses of action. The students learn not only more about a wide variety of interesting organizations but also these cases provide another opportunity for the students to develop their managerial competencies through active learning.

- Use of videos should be encouraged. This will help to provide students with an opportunity to improve their understanding of what managers actually do and also bring management to life. The videos are a motivating tool to stimulate student's interest and guides deeper analysis of the material covered in each chapter.

d. Measures of Student Learning outcomes includes:

- Direct measures: They are tangible, visible, self-explanatory evidence of exactly what students have and haven't learned (Suskie, 2004). It includes assessments such as Quizzes, Midterm, Final exams and Assignments. The assignment are usually in the form of group discussions, case studies, role plays, debates, presentations and projects.

- Indirect measures: They are signs of what students are learning (Suskie, 2004). It includes self assessment surveys.

- Rubrics: It is a flexible grading tool used to score performance assessment in a reliable, fair and valid manner. It is composed of dimensions for judging student performance. The scale for rating performances on each dimension and standards of excellence for specified performance levels is well defined. Rubric was used in the study for measuring the achievement of students learning outcome (SLO) using the combination of both direct and indirect assessments.

Data Collection

Source of data for the study includes both secondary and primary data. The secondary data required for study was obtained from publication in education sector, relevant business newspapers, magazine and journal and through surfing of various web sites. The necessary primary data for the study is obtained through structured questionnaire consisting of rating scale and by conducting interviews.

In order to eliminate the sampling frame errors and to ensure the representation of the population under study in the sample units, about equal respondents were approached at three academic levels: Freshman, sophomore and senior .The data were collected by self-administered questionnaires distributed to female business students of University College in the Eastern province of Kingdom of Saudi Arabia.

Instrument

The questionnaire was prepared in English. The experiential exercise Self assessment inventory measures characteristic that are representative of the core dimension of the five core managerial competencies as shown in Figure 3.1.

• **Communication Competency**
• **Planning and Administration Competency**
• **Team work Competency**
• **Multicultural Competency**
• **Self Management Competency**

Figure 3.1 The Dimensions Understudy

In total, there were 80 questions that were grouped into categories based on the selected five management competencies(Hellreigel,2002) .The 80 statements are list of characteristics that represents effective and experienced managers.

36

➤ Communication competency focuses on question 1-15. It contains 3 dimensions
- Informal communication refers to Q1-Q5
- Formal communication refers to Q6-Q10
- Negotiations refers to Q11-Q15

➤ Planning and Administration competency focus on questions Q1--15. It contains 4 dimensions
- Information gathering analysis, and problem solving refers to Q1-Q5
- Planning and organizing projects refers to Q6-Q10
- Time management refers to Q11-Q15
- Budgeting and financial management refers to Q16-Q20

➤ Teamwork competency focus on Q1-Q15. It has 3 dimensions
- Designing teams refers to Q1-Q5
- Creating a supportive team environment refers to Q6-10
- Managing team dynamics appropriately refers to Q11-15

➤ Multicultural competency focus on Q1-10. It has 2 dimensions
- Cultural knowledge and understanding refers to Q1-Q5
- Cultural openness and Understanding refers to Q6-Q10

➤ Self-Management competency focus on Q1-20 It has 4 dimensions
- Integrity and ethical conduct refers to Q1-Q5
- Personal drive & resilience refers to Q6-Q10
- Balancing work and life issues to Q11-Q15
- Self-awareness and development refers to Q 16-Q20

The main objective of this questionnaire was to determine the current level of student's attainment in these competencies .The various categories in the level of attainment are as follows:

Level of Attainment

1. I have very little relevant experience. I have not yet begun to develop this characteristic.

2. I think that I am weak in this characteristic. I have had relevant experience, but I have not performed well.

3. I think that I am about average on this characteristic. It will take a good deal of focused effort for me to be consistently effective.

4. I think that I am above average on this characteristic. I need to develop this characteristic further in order to be highly effective.

5. I think that I am outstanding on this characteristic. I need to maintain my strong effectiveness on this characteristic.

Each of the above five statements describes a level of attainment on a dimensions of the managerial competency The students have to self appraise how well they think each statement describes them. Next to each characteristic the students have to fill in the number corresponding to the level of attainment that applies best to them. Presenting an accurate self appraisal is important for understanding the current competencies and what they need to do to develop them further. The participants were politely approached and were invited to participate on a voluntary basis. Each questionnaire included a cover letter clarifying the nature and the purpose of the study. To ensure full understanding of the questions so as to get more accurate results the questionnaire was fully explained to the students in their classes. Once they had agreed to participate, the researcher then handed over the designated questionnaire to the participating respondents. The respondents were requested to present an accurate self-appraisal as it is important to understand their current competencies and what they need to do to develop them further. The researcher then left the respondent alone to answer the questionnaire and did not interfere in any way .This would help to avoid any potential bias such as the respondents feeling intimidated, threatened or being influenced by the researcher.On completion of questionnaire by respondents they were collected back by the researcher.

Sample

To achieve the objectives under study, the data were collected by self-administered questionnaires. As the study is undertaken by an individual researcher so it is not easy to contact all students. The convenient random sampling was so obtained. From 125 questionnaires distributed, 102 responses were received, thereby yielding a high response rate, a response rate considered sufficiently large for statistical reliability. This relatively high response rate was attributed to the self-administered approach undertaken in distributing questionnaires and approaching respondents. The collected data were edited, classified and analyzed using all type of relevant statically tools.

Statistical Measure

Data preparation begins with preliminary check of the entire filled up questionnaire for its completeness. The collected data was edited, coded, tabulated, grouped and organized according to the requirement of the study and then entered into SPSS (Statistical package for social sciences) for analysis. For analyzing the hypothesis, parametric as well as non-parametric test have been used in this research. To analyze the results, the hypothesis was tested using various statistical measures such as Percentage, Mean, Standard Deviation, Reliability, ANOVA and Correlation.

The standard deviation is the most frequently calculated measure of variability or dispersion in a set of data points. The standard deviation value represents the average distance of a set of scores from the mean or average score. Standard deviation and the normal curve descriptive statistic is the mean or average score in a set of data. The mean is a particularly informative measure of the "central tendency" of the variable if it is reported along with its confidence intervals .

Correlation is a measure of the relation between two or more variables. Correlation coefficients can range from -1.00 to +1.00. The value of -1.00 represents a perfect negative correlation while a value of +1.00 represents a perfect positive correlation. A value of 0.00 represents a lack of correlation. The most widely used type of correlation coefficient is Pearson r, also called linear or product moment correlation. Pearson correlation determines the extent to which values of the two variables are "proportional" to each other. The value of correlation (correlation coefficient) does not depend on the specific measurement units used. Data analysis was carried out by using Statistical Package for Social Scientists (SPSS) for Windows were performed through SPSS 19 and MS Excel 2010.

Limitations of the Study

All efforts have been made to ensure that the research is designed and conducted to optimize the ability to achieve the research objective. However there are some constraints that do not validate the research but need to be acknowledged.

- This study is restricted to the female business students of   University College in the Eastern province of Kingdom of Saudi Arabia.

- A limited number of samples could only be studied and hence the results would not be as accurate as that of population survey in education sectors.
- The study is based on the response of the students who are highly subjective in nature and hence generalization made may not be totally true.

Chapter 4

Models and Philosophies of Competencies

Defining Competencies

Competencies are the abilities to use knowledge and other capabilities, which is necessary for   accomplishment of a task in the business process. McClelland (1973) is credited with initiating the idea of "competency" and implementing it into the human resource literature (Dubois, 1993). Boyatzis (1982) is credited with popularizing the term in his book "The Competent Manager" .The competency is a blend of a motive, trait, skill, social role and relevant knowledge.

Cooper and Graham (2001) identified 57 core competencies requires by workers. The traits and motives identified as critical component for success in an HR career were adaptability, proactivity, respect, conscientiousness, courage , integrity, energy level and self-esteem . While the four categories of skills were cognitive, communication ,collaborative and consulting. The research published over the last 30 years shows that outstanding leaders, managers, advanced professionals and people in main jobs, need three clusters of behavioral habits namely (1) expertise and experience (2) knowledge (3) basic cognitive competencies (Bray et al., 1974; Boyatzis, 1982; Kotter, 1982; Campbell et al., 1970; Spencer and Spencer, 1993; Goleman, 1998; Goleman et al., 2002). Competencies are also considered as behavioral approach to emotional, social and cognitive intelligence   weather it is bank executives, public school principals, research and development managers or military pilots. There were no significant differences between male and female leaders in their demonstration of emotional and social intelligence competencies (Margaret M. Hopkins etal 2008).

Research studies by Liu Yah Olan (2012) on mid-level managers in Sichuan, Wittaya Chansiri (2009) on public university supporting-line administrators in Thailand, Neda Tiraieyari etal (2010) investigation on Malaysian extension workers at the department of agriculture, Rubin Pillay (2008), analysis of hospital managers in South Africa, Kak etal, (2001) studies on Healthcare Providers and Candace Blayney (2009) on Canadian hotel general managers has depicted that the competencies required by employee are job and sector specific.The degree of competency development during the management program enhances career advancement in general and develop competencies like planning, networking, system thinking and using technology in particular . According to Richard E. Boyatzis, 2006 competencies can be developed .

Core Managerial Competencies

Managerial competencies "are sets of knowledge, skills, behaviors, and attitudes that an individual needs to be effective in a wide range of managerial jobs and various type of organizations. The six core competencies that managers need in order to succeed are shown in Figure 4.1. they are (a) Communication Competency, (b) Planning and Administration Competency, (c) Teamwork Competency, (d) Multicultural Competency, (e) Self-Management Competency. (Hellriegel etal 2008). These competencies are transferable from one organization to other.

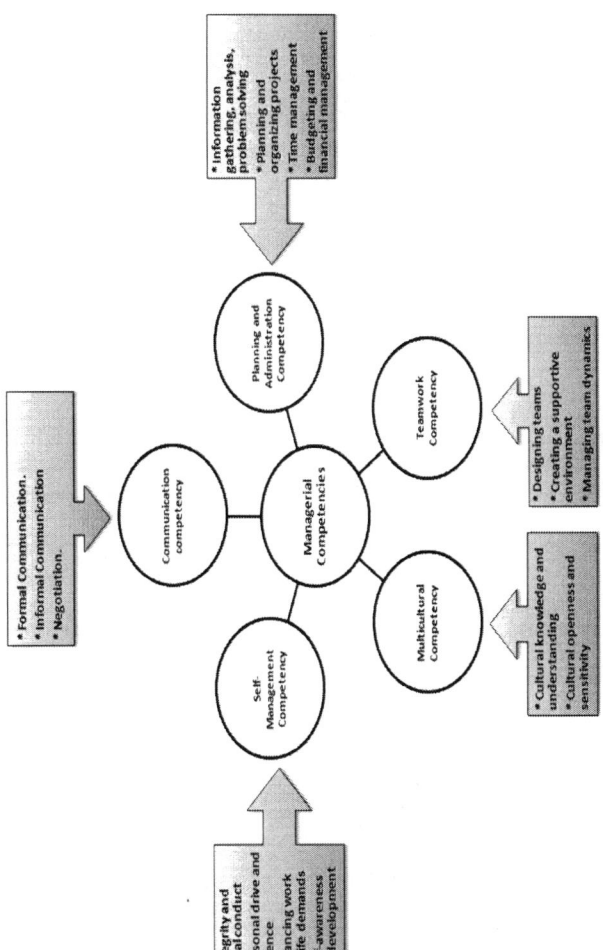

Figure 4.1 The Core Managerial Competencies

44

Communication competency

Communication competency is "the ability to interact with others"(Spitzberg.1984). This competence is best understood as "a situational ability to set realistic and appropriate goals and to maximize their achievement by using knowledge of self, others and environment to generate adaptive communication performances". Communication competencies has been found to be related with effective management .It strengthens the establishment for thriving management. Communication is so basic and primary that managers sometimes forget its significance to effective management .Competent managers not only lead others, but also listen and share their ideas. The dimension of this competency involves listening, informing others, fostering open channels and negotiating with others. The flow of information freely in all directions is the most important parameter in an organization. Mastering the communication competency greatly expands the manager's influence and effectiveness. Number of cases and experiential exercises help students ascertain the importance of sharing information with others and of developing a culture in which they can openly share information.

Planning and administration competency

Planning and administration competency involves deciding what tasks need to be done. It is also about determining how they can be done and allocating resources to enable them to be done. Last but not the least it involves monitoring progress to ensure that they are done. Competent managers recognize the fact that the tool and techniques that worked well in the past may sometimes no longer serve the needs of an organization.

This competency involves the regular review of the changing internal and external needs of the organization as well as altering the changing competencies of employees. Competent managers lead by setting clear and challenging goals , proper planning , coordinating and monitoring . They also step in to help resolve problem as and when it arises. However, sometimes tasks may be neglected when managers spend too much time dealing with insignificant problems. This holds true also for the employees who may sometimes waste time because of inadequate control, poor guidance and slow decision making. Students can learn how effective managers use the planning and administration competency to create organizations that are responsive to customer demands and needs through a series of examples and cases.

Strategic action competency

Strategic action competency involves "understanding the overall mission and values of the company and ensuring that your actions and those of the people you manage are aligned with them". (Hellriegel et al., 2008) Competent managers prepare unique strategies to guide an organization to achieve competitive advantage. Strategies are the major courses of action that are selected and implemented to achieve goals. Risks accompany all strategic decisions, but the competent managers minimize those risks by crafting contingency plans. Students get a feel of these competencies by discussion that demonstrates how managers of many types of organization actually craft, develop and implement creative and competent strategies. This enables strategic thinking among these students.

Teamwork competency

Teamwork competency requires accomplishing tasks through small groups of people who are collectively responsible and whose work is interdependent. It requires close collaboration, leadership and constant information sharing. The dimensions of teamwork competency involves creating a healthy environment by forming give-and –take relationships, striving to enhance mutual understanding and respect, acknowledging the needs and feeling of others and managing conflict productively. Competent managers are able to not only cultivate an active network of relationships but also to work well in diverse teams. They form and staff teams with the right combination of talents and monitor its performance. They encourage team members and make the availability of all the resources they need in order to be effective and to achieve their organizational goals.

Multicultural Competency

Multicultural competency is the ability to foster relationship with the people of host nations and understand the perceptions of host nation's culture and its social systems. Hellriegel et al (2008) defines it as "performing managerial work for an organization that utilizes human, financial and material resources from multiple countries and serves markets that span multiple cultures".
Competent managers stay updated of important trends among and across nations that have potential impacts on their organizations. They also diagnose how well their organizations are performing in global market. This competency challenges students to recognize the effect and impact of global trends on an organization's plans and growth. The challenges of global expansion and operation in various countries demand that students question their own leadership styles, values and management practices. The main factors for doing successful business globally are being sensitive to key

cultural, political and economic differences in countries in which an organization operates and assessing the consequences of those differences for the organization.

Self-management competency

Self-management competency refers to taking responsibility for your life at work and beyond. (Hellriegel et al 2002). Competent managers know that self-awareness is a crucial point to view the operation as well as his or her role in that organization. Identification of one's strength and developmental needs is the first important step in the process of learning to manage and lead others. Presentation, experiential exercises and cases on self-management competency assists students in identifying their own strength and developmental needs in leadership, motivation, ethics and other areas. The students gain an appreciation for the importance of continual self-assessment throughout their careers.

Competencies of 21st century

A competency is defined as a capability or ability and is a set of related but different sets of behavior organized around an underlying construct, which we call the "intent". The behaviors are alternate manifestations of the intent, as suitable in various context. The underlying intent is to understand the person. A theory of performance is the basis for the concept of competency as shown in Figure 4.2. According to the basic contingency theory optimum performance is a product of person's talent , the job demands and the organizational environment (Boyatzis, 1982).

- The person's talent is all about his values, vision, knowledge, competencies, career stage, interests and style.

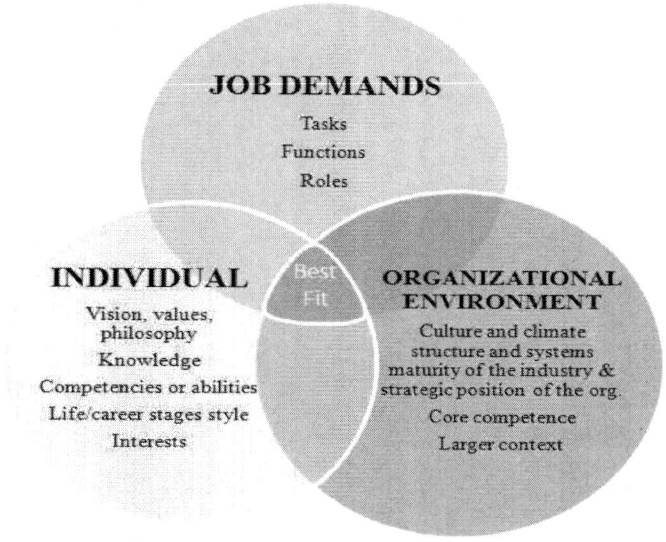

JOB DEMANDS

Tasks
Functions
Roles

ORGANIZATIONAL ENVIRONMENT

Culture and climate
structure and systems
maturity of the industry &
strategic position of the org.
Core competence
Larger context

INDIVIDUAL

Vision, values,
philosophy
Knowledge
Competencies or abilities
Life/career stages style
Interests

Best Fit

Figure 4.2 The Basic Contingency Theory

49

- The job demands are the roles, responsibilities and tasks needed to be performed in an organization to achieve its goals.
- Organizational environment include culture and climate, structure , systems, maturity of the industry ,strategic positioning ,the economic, political, social, environmental and cultural background surrounding the organization.

Research available over the last 30 years or so shows us that extraordinary leaders, advanced professionals and people in key jobs require three clusters of competencies namely:

- Expertise and experience
- Knowledge
- Cognitive Competency

There are three clusters of competencies differentiating outstanding from average performers in many countries of the world (Bray et al., 1974; Boyatzis, 1982; Kotter, 1982; Luthans et. al., 1988; Howard and Bray, 1988; Campbell et al., 1970; Spencer and Spencer, 1993; Goleman, 1998; Goleman et al., 2002). They are as follows :
- The cognitive competencies
- The emotional intelligence
- The social intelligence competencies

Developing Competencies

The behavioral approach one of the most accepted approach to talent focus on the development of human talent during the adulthood. Research has proved that people can change their behavior, moods and self image by

- effects of psychotherapy (Hubble et. al., 1999)
- self-help programs (Kanfer and Goldstein, 1991)
- cognitive behavior therapy (Barlow,1988)
- training programs (Morrow et al., 1997)
- education (Pascarella and Terenzini, 1991; Winter et al., 1981)

But most of the study are focused on a single characteristic such as sobriety, specific anxiety, characteristics determined by the assessment instrument . There are also few studies showing sustained improvements in the sets of desirable behavior that lead to extra ordinary performance. The typical training programs usually starts with great enthusiasm but within months it drops drastically (Campbell et. al., 1970). The Consortium on Research on Emotional Intelligence in organizations could only identify fifteen programs to improve emotional intelligence that showed impact on job outcomes(Cherniss and Adler, 2000). The few published studies have shown an overall improvement of about 10 percent in emotional intelligence abilities in a period of three to eighteen months of subsequent training (Boyatzis, 2006). A sequence of longitudinal studies underway at the Weatherhead School of Management of Case Western Reserve University have shown that people can change on emotional and social intelligence competencies (Boyatzis et al., 2002). The upgrading lasted for years that it differentiates outstanding performers in management and professions.

 A real learning comes from thinking about the challenging experience over the period of time. Taking a challenging project doesn't assure learning but people willingness to play a constructive role in the project is highly significant. Regardless of when , where or how people develop these competencies , they should be able to use them in future jobs that they can't yet even imagine holding or that may not even exist today. One way to enhance managerial competencies is by participating in extracurricular activities, which help to expand competencies such as communication and team work that often can be transferred to a diversity of jobs . Another way is by taking appropriate courses and volunteering to take part in international clubs and associations. This helps in broadening knowledge of other countries and building multicultural competency. Holding an office in a volunteer organizations or taking responsibility for organizing a community event can also be done to enhance the planning and administration competency. The campus recruiters these days pay a great deal of attention to the students involvement in extracurricular activities   rather than just looking at grade point average .

Chapter 5

Conceptual Issues Impacting Learning in Business Education

How people learn

A thriving organization or renowned manager is always characterized by their ability to learn. However it is astonishing that the ability to learn which is extensively so significant receives very minute consideration from the organization. There is a kind of fatalism regarding understanding the learning process itself. The business schools need to create awareness to show the ways in which the learning process and individual learning style affect managerial decision making , problem solving and organizational learning.

The model which describes how people learn is popularly called as the Experiential learning model (ETM). Experiential learning is "the process whereby knowledge is created through the transformation of experience. The knowledge is the result of product of grasping and transforming experience"(Kolb 1984).Experiential learning model is a combination of holistic model of the learning process and multilinear model of adult development. Both of these models are consistent with how people learn, how they grow and how they develop. The theory is known as "Experiential Learning" to stress the vital role that 'experience" plays in the learning process. It also highlights the distinguishing factors from cognitive learning theories, which aptly emphasize cognition over affect and behavioral learning theories that disallow any role for subjective experience in the learning process. One more reason for the theory to be called "experiential" lies in the intellectual roots of learning and development works of Dewey's, Lewin's and Piaget. (Kolb, 1984).

Learning is   visualized as a four stage cycle as shown in figure 5.1. The certain abilities that are required in order to gain genuine knowledge from an experience are:

- Concrete Experience (CE):The learner must be willing to be actively involved in the new experience without bias
- Reflective Observation (RO):The learner must be able to reflect on and observe these experience from many perspectives
- Abstract Conceptualization (AC):The learner must possess and use analytical skills to conceptualize the experience into logical sound theories
- Active Experimentation (AE): The learner must possess decision making and problem solving skills in order to use the new ideas gained from the experience

The Experiential learning Model describes two dialectically related modes as shown in Figure 5.2

(a) Grasping experience comprising of Concrete Experience (CE) and Abstract Conceptualization (AC) and

(b) Transforming experience comprising of Reflective Observation (RO) and Active Experimentation (AE)

According to the four-stage learning cycle immediate or concrete experiences are the basis for both observation and reflection. The reflections are converted into abstract concepts from which new implications for action can be derived. The results of these can be easily tested and serve as guides in generating new experiences. The learning

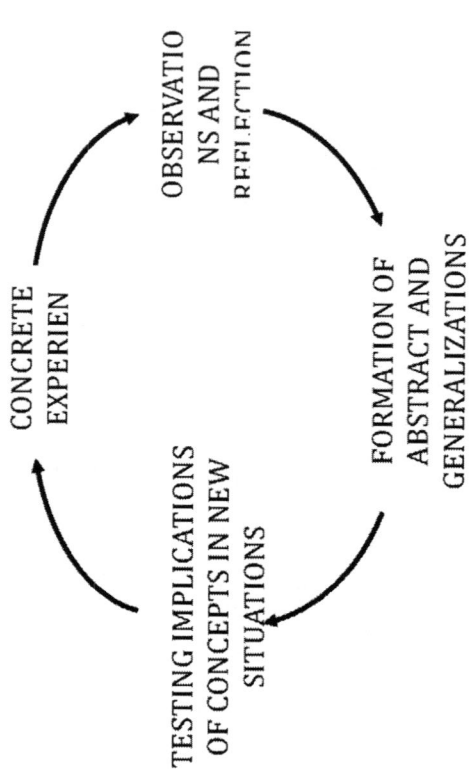

Figure 5.1 The Experiential Learning Cycle

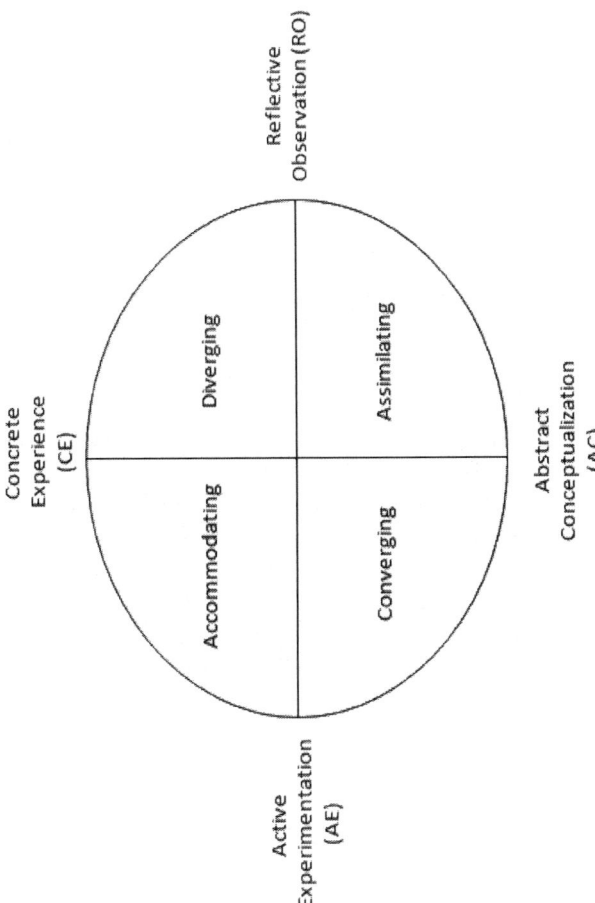

Figure 5.2 The Experiential Leaning Cycle and Basic Learning Styles (Kolb, 1984)

need abilities   are polar opposites.   The learner must continually opt for learning abilities he or she will utilize in a specific learning situation.

In grasping experience most of us recognize new information during experiencing the concrete, tangible, felt qualities of the world, relying on our senses and immersing ourselves in concrete reality .While others may likely grasp, new information through abstract conceptualization which may involve thinking, analyzing and planning to a certain extent than using sensation as a channel.

Similarly, in transforming or processing experience some of us tend to carefully watch others who are involved in the experience and reflect on what happens, while others choose to jump right in and start doing things. The watchers usually support reflective observation, while the doer's active experimentation. Therefore in the course of learning one moves in varying degrees from the actor to observer, from specific involvement to general analytic detachment. The experiences are translated into concepts which in turn are used as channels in choice of new experience.

This 'cycle of learning' is the fundamental principle in the experiential learning theory and classically expressed as four-stage cycle of learning, a cycle of experiencing, reflecting, thinking and acting. The 'immediate or concrete experiences' provide a basis for 'observations and reflections'. These 'observations and reflections' are assimilated into 'abstract concepts' producing new implications for action which can be 'actively tested' in turn creating new experiences.

Each dimension of the learning process presents us with a choice. For example it is impossible, to drive a car (Concrete Experience) and analyze a driver's manual (Abstract Conceptualization) simultaneously. We resolve this conflict between concrete and abstract and between active or reflective in some patterned ways called as "learning styles."

Individual Learning Styles

Most people develop learning styles based on their learning abilities, the hereditary, past life experiences and present environment. Some people develop minds that do extremely well at absorbing disparate facts into coherent theories , yet these same people are incapable of or uninterested in working out hypotheses from their theories . Others are logical geniuses but find it unfeasible to engross and surrender them to an experience and so on. A mathematician may give importance on abstracts concepts, while a poet may worth concrete experience more highly, a manager may be principally concerned with the active application of ideas while a naturalist may build up his observational skills highly. Each solely develops a learning style that has some strength and weakness.

 There are four prevailing learning styles: Diverging, Assimilating, Converging, and Accommodating. These are based on Learning style inventory (LSI) scores obtained from both research and clinical observation (Kolb, 1984, 1999a, 1999b).

> Diverging
- Concrete Experience (CE) and Reflective Observation (RO) are their dominant learning abilities.
- People who possess this learning style are best at viewing concrete situations from many different points of view.
- They also have broad cultural interests and like to gather information, they are interested in people, are inclined towards imagination and emotion, cultural aspects and arts.

- It is known as "Diverging" as the person with this style performs better in context , like "brainstorming" which call for generation of ideas.
- In formal learning situations, people prefer to work in groups, listen with an open mind and receive personalized feedback.

➢ Assimilating
- Abstract Conceptualization (AC) and Reflective Observation (RO) are their dominant learning abilities.
- Here the People are best at understanding a wide range of information and putting into concise, logical form and find it more important that a theory have logical soundness than practical value.
- They are less focused on people and more interested in ideas and abstract concepts. So this learning style is important for effectiveness in information and science careers.
- In formal learning situations, these people prefer readings, lectures, exploring analytical models and having time to think things through.

➢ Converging
- Abstract Conceptualization (AC) and Active Experimentation (AE) are their dominant learning abilities.
- People with this learning style are good at finding practical uses for ideas and theories, have the ability to solve problems and make decisions based on finding solutions to problems.
- They prefer to deal with technical tasks and problems rather than with social and interpersonal issues. So these learning skills are important for effectiveness in specialist and technology careers.
- In formal learning situations, people prefer to experiment with new ideas, simulations, laboratory assignments and practical applications.

- ➢ Accommodating
- Concrete Experience (CE) and Active Experimentation (AE) are their dominant learning style.
- People with this learning style, have the ability to learn from primarily "hand-on" experience. They usually enjoy carrying out plans and involve themselves in new and challenging experiences.
- Their tendency may be to act on "gut" feelings rather than on logical analysis. In solving problems, they rely more heavily on people for information than on their own technical analysis. This style is important for effectiveness in action-oriented careers such as marketing or sales.
- In formal learning situations, people prefer to work with others to get assignments done, set goals, do field work, and test out different approaches in completing a project.

Behavior and Learning Styles

The discussed patterns of behavior related with the four basic learning styles are shown constantly at various levels of behavior. Figure 5.3 summarizes the characteristics of learning styles at five particular levels of behavior such as:

- Personality types
- Early educational specialization
- Professional career
- Current job role
- Adaptive competencies

The Accommodating learning style is the most extraverted sensing type, which have educational backgrounds in Business and Management. It

Behavior level	Diverging	Assimilating	Converging	Accommodating
Personality	Introverted	Introverted	Extraverted	Extraverted
Types	Feeling	Intuition	Thinking	Sensation
Educational	Art, English	Economics	Engineering	Business
Specialization	History, psychology	Mathematics , sociology, chemistry	physical sciences	Management
professional	Social Service	Sciences	Technology	Organizations
Career	Arts Communication	Research Information	Economics Environment	Business
Current jobs	Personal jobs	Information jobs	Technical jobs	Executive jobs
Adaptive	Valuing	Thinking	Decision	Action
Competencies	Skills	Skills	Skills	Skills

Figure 5.3 Relations Between the Basic Learning Styles and Five Levels of Behavior

characterizes people with careers in organizations such as management, finance, educational administration and doing business in marketing, government, human resources .Executive jobs like general management, which needs a strong orientation to task accomplishment and decision making in uncertain circumstances also require an accommodating learning style. This learning style encompasses a set of competencies that can best be termed "Acting skills "comprising of Leadership, Initiative and Action. Experiential Learning Theory is a holistic theory of learning that identifies learning style differences among different academic specialties. It has been used as a structure for innovation in business education and includes research on learning styles and environments, curriculum design and experiential learning (e.g., Boyatzis, Cowen, & Kolb, 1995; Lengnick-Hall & Sanders, 1997).

New Trends in Experiential Learning Theory:

Integrated learning is a new direction for Experiential Learning Theory. It is conceptualized as a standard learning cycle where the learner gets the base of experiencing, reflecting, thinking and acting. There are three orders of learning styles as shown in Figure 5.4 .The first includes the basic learning styles - Diverging, Assimilating, Converging and Accommodating. People with a basic learning style resolve the dialectics of the learning process by specializing in some modes at the expense of others.

The second-order learning styles represent learning orientations that integrate one of the two dialectics of the learning process. It about combining the abilities of two basic learning styles. Abbey, Hunt, and Weiser (1985) and Hunt (1987) call these as leNortherner, Easterner, Southerner and Westerner learningstyles.

Learning styles	Developed modes	Underdeveloped modes
First-Order Learning Styles		
Diverging	CE, RO	AC, AE
Assimilating	AC, RO	CE, AE
Converging	AC, AE	CE, RO
Accommodating	CE, AE	AC, RO
Second-Order Learning Styles		
Northerner	CE, RO, AE	AC
Easterner	CE, AC, RO	AE
Westerner	CE, AC, AE	RO
Southerner	AC, RO, AE	CE
Third-Order Learning Styles		
Balanced Profiles	CE, AC, RO, AE	None

Notes: CE= Concrete Experience, AC= Abstract Conceptualization, RO= Reflective Observation, AE= Active Experimentation

Figure 5.4 Learning Modes and First, Second, and Third-Order Learning Styles

In the third-order of learning styles we have three balanced learning profiles all three balanced profiles are manifestations of integrated learning in the sense that people with these styles learn in a holistic way, utilizing effectively the abilities associated with all four learning modes. The slight difference between the three balanced profiles is that the first among them emphasizes the Concrete Experience/ Abstract Conceptualization dimension more than the Reflective Observation/ Active Experimentation dimension, while the inverse is the case with the second profile. The balanced profile emphasis equally on both the dimensions(Kolb etal 2005).

Learning styles and Business Education

Research on learning styles of managers shows them possessing very strong active experimentation skills but weak reflective observation skills which is reverse for the Business school's faculty members. The manager who comes to the university for career education experiences a culture shock as he gets   rewarded for reflections and analysis rather than concrete goal directed actions . He has to transform himself from manager who used to "acts before he thinks"   to be a student who "thinks before he acts". He has to become accustomed to a slow world of generalities.

To bridge this gap in learning style the management educator must respond to pragmatic demands for relevance and application of knowledge while encouraging the reflective examination of experience that is necessary to refine old theories and to build new ones. Managerial education will not be improved by eliminating theoretical analysis or relevant case problems. Improvement will come through integration of scholarly and practical learning styles and by applying directly the experiential learning models in classroom.

In traditional methods the conflict between scholar and practioner learning style is exaggerated because the material to be taught is filtered through learning style of the faculty member in his lecturers. In the experiential process this filtration process does not take place because both teacher and student are observers of immediate experiences which they both interpret according to their own learning styles.

There are two goals in the experiential learning process. One is to learn the in depth of a particular subject .The other goal is to learn about ones strength and weakness as a learner-" learning how to learn from experience". When the process works well, these budding managers finish their educational experience not only with new intellectual insights, but also with an understanding of their own learning style. This understanding of learning strength and weakness helps in the application of what has been learned and provides a framework for continuing learning on the job. Day to day experience becomes a focus for testing and exploring new ideas and it becomes an integral and explicit part of work itself.

Experiential learning can be divided into two major categories:
- Field-based experiences
- Classroom-based learning

Field-based learning is the oldest and most established form of experiential learning, which has been integrated into higher education in the 1930s. Field-based learning consists of internships, practicums, cooperative education, and service learning (Lewis & Williams, 1994).

Classroom-based experiential learning can take a multitude of forms, including role-playing, games, case studies, simulations, presentations and group work. The experiential learning in the classroom has been growing in breadth and depth since 'active learning' was recommended as one of the seven 'principles of good practice' for excellence in undergraduate education (Lewis & Williams, 1994).

The case study method helps to learn analytical and problem solving skills by presenting a case about people in an organization who are facing a problem or decisions involving real people in an organization .Case may be based on actual events involving real people in an organization or may be fictional. In solving a problem students are generally required to use a rational problem solving process that includes:

1. Restating important facts
2. Drawing inferences from the facts
3. Stating the problems
4. Developing alternatives solutions and then stating the consequences of each
5. Determining and supporting a course of action

Like the case method, business games are intended to develop or refine problem solving and decision making skills However this technique tends to focus primarily on business management decisions such as maximizing profit. Business games, particularly computer simulations of the organizations and industry are widely used in business schools .Another type of simulations used in management development program and assessment centre is the "in basket exercise". The goal of this technique is to assess the trainee's ability to establish priorities, to gather relevant information and make decisions.

In Role playing techniques the students are presented with an organizational situation, assigned roles or character of a situation and asked to act out the role with one or more students. The role play offers student an opportunity for self discovery and learning. The students should have opportunity to role play both manager and subordinate roles, in order to understand some of the dynamics of this situation as well as practice feedback sessions following the role play.

Behavior Modeling is based on the principle of social learning theory that suggests that many of our behavioral patterns are learned from observing others. This theory forms the basis for behavior modeling .The students observe a model performing a target behavior correctly usually on video or DVD .This is followed by discussion of the key components of the behavior, practicing the target behavior through role playing and receiving feedback . This is widely used for interpersonal skills training.

Learning styles and Managerial Problem Solving

Comparison of the experiential learning model with a typical model of problem solving process is shown in the Figure 5.5. It matches to the learning style strength of the four major learning style described earlier. The accommodator's problem solving strength lie in executing solutions and initiating problem and finding based on some goals or model about how things should be. The diverter's problem solving potency lie in identifying the multitude of possible problems and opportunities that exist in reality. The assimilator stand out in the abstract model building that is necessary to choose a priority problem and alternative solutions. The converter's strong point lies in the evaluation of solution consequences and solution selection.

Like individuals, organizations learn and develop a distinctive learning style. They can do so through their transactions with the environment and through their choice of how to relate to the environment. This has come to be known as the open system view of organization. Since many organizations are large and complex, the environment they relate to become highly differentiated and diverse. The way the organization adapts to this external environment is to differentiate itself into units each of which deals with just one part of the firm's external conditions. Marketing and sales face problems associated

.

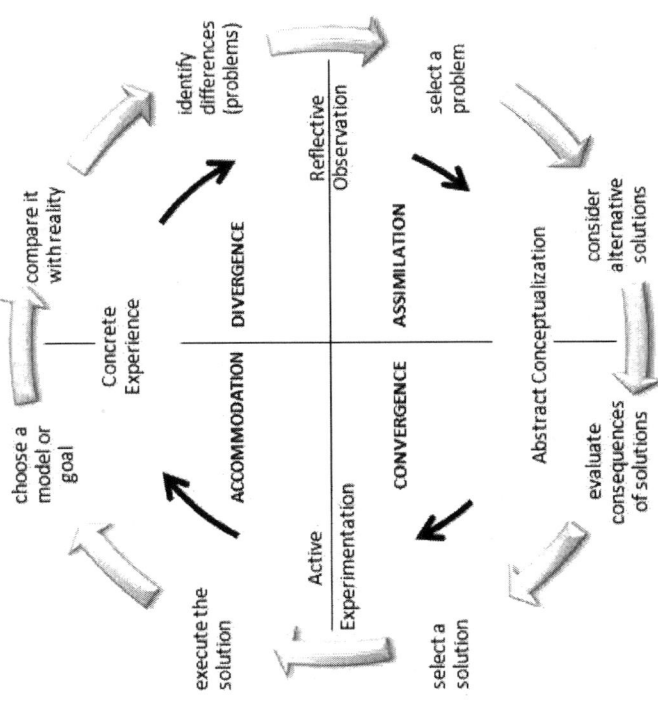

Figure 5.5 Learning styles and Managerial Problem Solving

with market customers and competitors. Research deals with academic and technological worlds. Production deals with production equipment and raw materials sources. Personnel and labor relations deal with labor market and so on. Because of this need to relate to different aspects of the environment , the different units of the firm develop characteristic ways of thinking and working together , different styles of decision styles of decision making and problem solving these units select and shape managers to solve problems and make decisions in the way their environment demands (David Kolb 1976). If the organization is thought of as a learning system then each of the differentiated units that is charged with adapting to the changes of one segment of the environment can be thought of as having a characteristic learning style that is best suited to meet those environmental demands. Thus the Business education should introduce the concept of learning space as a frame work for understanding the interface between student learning styles and the institutional learning environment (Kolb & Kolb 1999).

Chapter 6

Assessing the Competencies

In recognition of the importance of helping Business students develop competencies, the American Association of Collegiate School of Management acknowledged competencies in their eligibility procedures and standard for management accreditation (AACSB International 2006). The competencies understudy was at par with them.For assessing the achievement of the students learning outcomes data analysis was carried out using Statistical Package for Social Scientists (SPSS) for windows. Developing and measuring competencies in management education is highly challenging task and the present research was successful in achieving the following objectives:

A. To determine the current level of student's attainment in the core managerial competencies

B. To analyze the impact of Academic year on core managerial competencies

C. To analyze the impact of core managerial competencies on Grades of the students

D. To determine the achievement of the students learning outcomes using rubric

Student's Attainment in the Core Managerial Competencies

To determine the current level of student's attainment in the core managerial competencies, a pilot study was conducted to verify the usability of the instrument. The finding for core managerial competencies demonstrated the reliability and the validity of the instrument and is depicted in Figure 6.1. The closer cronbach's alpha coefficient is to 1.0, the greater would be the internal consistency of the items in the scale. George and Mallery (2003) gives the following rules of thumb:

> .9: Excellent; > .8: Good; > .7: Acceptable;

> .6: Questionable ;> .5: Poor; < .5: Unacceptable

Variables	Communication competency	Planning and administration competency	Team work competency	Multicultural competency	Self competency
Cronbach's Alpha	.799	.760	.678	.705	.775

Figure 6.1 Reliability Statistics for the Core Managerial Competencies

The core competencies under study include communication, planning and administration, team work, multicultural and self competency. The cronbach's alpha values are greater than 0.6 for communication, planning and administration, team work, multicultural and self management competencies, which shows that the test conducted was reliable and valid.

Descriptive Analysis of Core Managerial Competencies

The summary of descriptive analysis in terms of mean and standard deviation for the core managerial competencies are shown in Figure 6.2. Since the questionnaire used 5 point scale, average mean score of 3 indicates a moderate tendency on that variable. Scores around 4 indicate a fairly good degree of existence .Here the competency score for communication was 3.91. This score was the highest among all the other competencies under study. This is followed by self management competency score which was 3.78. The team work score was 3.59, the multicultural 3.55 while planning and administration was 3.16. All the scores indicate the existence of good degree of level of attainment of the core managerial competencies. The mean scores of each variable are graphical represented in Figure 6.3.

Variables	Mean	Std. Deviation
Communication	3.91	.46
Planning and Administration	3.16	.31
Teamwork	3.59	.37
Multicultural	3.55	.40
Self Management	3.78	.39

Figure 6.2 Descriptive Analysis of Core Managerial Competencies

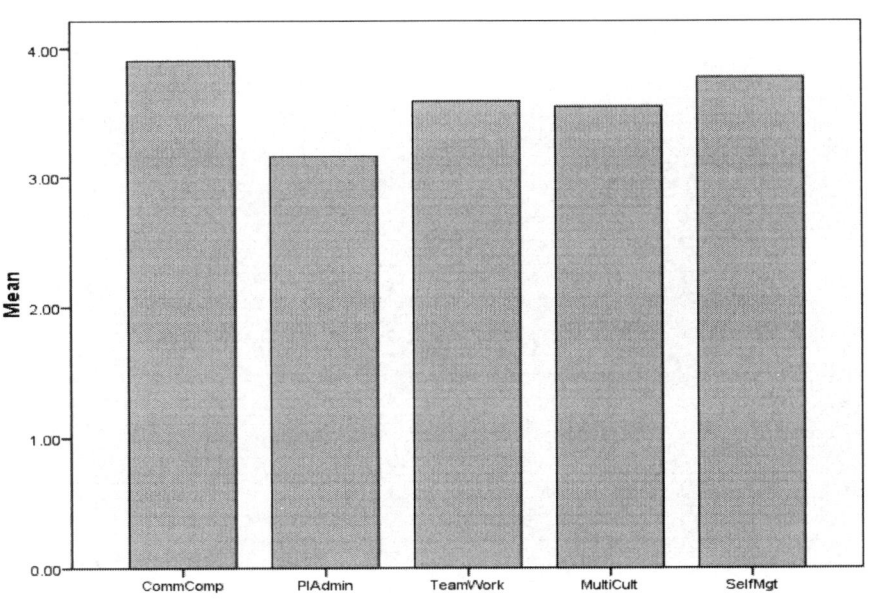

Figure 6.3 Graphical representation of Mean of Core Managerial competencies

Impact of the Academic Year On Managerial Competencies

To study the impact of the academic year on managerial competencies descriptive analysis of the managerial competencies was carried out. The summary of descriptive analysis in terms of mean and standard deviation for

Competencies and Academic Year		Mean	Std. Deviation	Std. Error
Communication	Freshman	3.7073	.47932	.07486
	Sophomore	3.9650	.34260	.05417
	Seniors	4.1810	.33276	.07261
	Total	3.9059	.43745	.04331
Planning and Administration	Freshman	3.0732	.36710	.05733
	Sophomore	3.2063	.25475	.04028
	Seniors	3.2595	.22058	.04813
	Total	3.1637	.30662	.03036
Team Work	Freshman	3.5398	.42159	.06584
	sophomore	3.6550	.26447	.04182
	Seniors	3.5587	.26706	.05828
	Total	3.5889	.33826	.03349
Multi Cultural	Freshman	3.3610	.41405	.06466
	Sophomore	3.6750	.34623	.05474
	Seniors	3.6619	.32012	.06986
	Total	3.5461	.39719	.03933
Self Management	Freshman	3.6159	.44517	.06952
	Sophomore	3.8925	.31593	.04995
	Seniors	3.8762	.29649	.06470
	Total	3.7779	.39026	.03864

Figure 6.4 Descriptive Analysis of the Managerial Competencies with Academic Year

The core managerial competencies with respect to academic year namely freshman, sophomore and seniors students are shown in Figure 6.4.

For communication competencies, the senior students had the highest score of 4.18, this was followed by sophomore students with 3.9650. In the planning and administration competencies the seniors students had highest score of 3.2595, followed by the students of sophomore with 3.206. In the team work competency again the sophomore students had high scores of 3.6550 followed by the senior's students with 3.5587. The multicultural competency was also highest in sophomore students with score of 3.6750 and followed by seniors with 3.6619. The self management competency was high attainment in sophomore with score of 3.8925 followed by again seniors with 3.8762. The graphical representation of academic year namely freshman, sophomore and seniors with communication competency, planning and administration, team work, multicultural and self management is shown in Figure 6.5.

Of all the students in various academic years under study, the freshman students being new to the college environment their attainment of the competencies were lower compared to the sophomore and the senior's .The students at the sophomore level performed extremely well in all the competencies under study .These students are in second year of the college study. Their attainment of all the managerial competencies under study is highly significant followed by the senior students. The senior students are the students in the fourth year .There exists only slight difference between the attainment of competencies in the sophomore and the senior level students. The senior's level students scored the highest in the communication competencies, which means that as the students gain more experience their communication competency improves. The lowest attainment of competencies among the students was that of Planning and administration competency.

Figure 6.5 Graphical representation of Communication, Planning and administration, Team work, Multicultural and Self management Competency with Academic Year

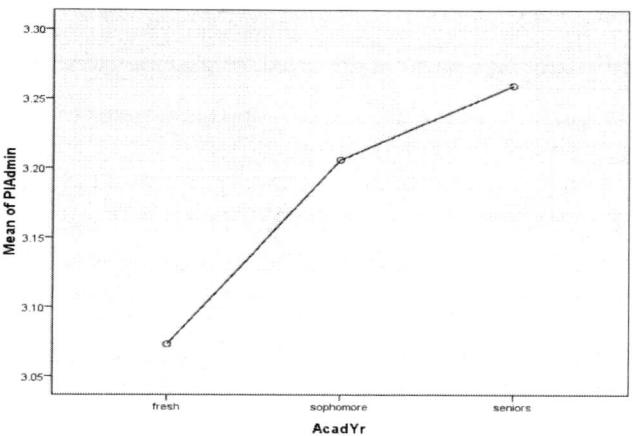

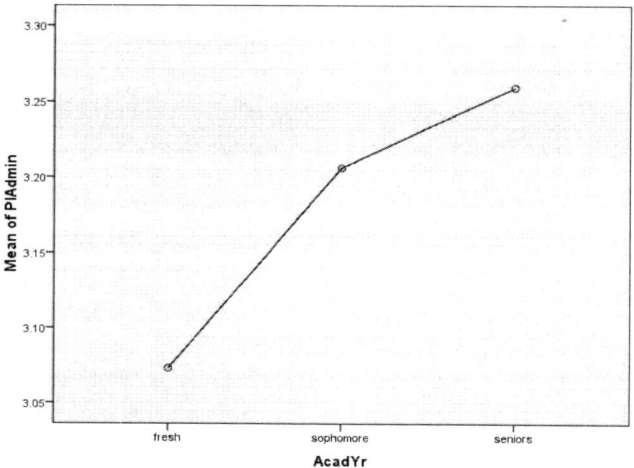

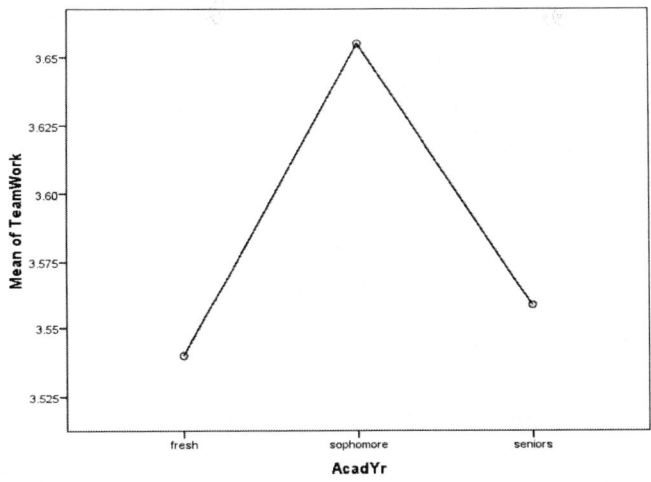

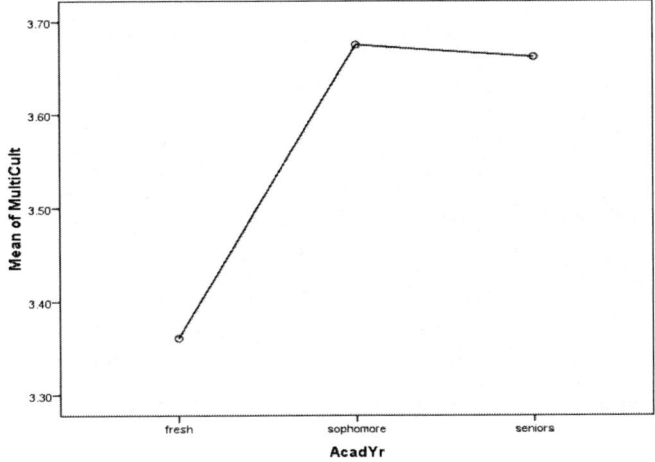

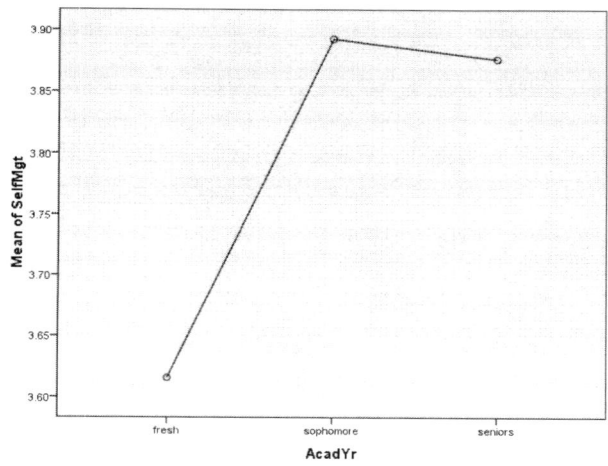

Analysis of variance (ANOVA)

In statistics, one-way analysis of variance (ANOVA) is a technique used to compare means of three or more samples using the F distribution. The ANOVA tests the null hypothesis when the samples in two or more groups are drawn from populations with the same mean values. The ANOVA produces an F-statistic, the ratio of the variance calculated among the means to the variance within the samples.

The ANOVA results in Figure 6.6 between groups and within groups show that communication competency among students has significant results for three different levels of studies; communication competency is highest for senior students, followed by sophomore and then freshman students.

The multicultural competency had also significant results where again sophomore students were best and freshman were found to be less competent. The results for Teamwork competency among students were not very significant. The Self-management competency among students were found to be significant at different levels of academic year and so also the planning and administration competencies were found to be significant at different levels of academic year.

ANOVA		Sum of Squares	df	Mean Square	F	Sig.
Communication	Between Groups	3.345	2	1.673	10.361	.000
	Within Groups	15.982	99	.161		
	Total	19.328	101			
Planning and Administration	Between Groups	.601	2	.301	3.346	.039
	Within Groups	8.895	99	.090		
	Total	9.496	101			
Team Work	Between Groups	.293	2	.146	1.286	.281
	Within Groups	11.264	99	.114		
	Total	11.556	101			
Multi Cultural	Between Groups	2.351	2	1.176	8.569	.000
	Within Groups	13.582	99	.137		
	Total	15.933	101			
Self Management	Between Groups	1.805	2	.902	6.580	.002
	Within Groups	13.578	99	.137		
	Total	15.383	101			

Figure 6.6 ANOVA Test for Managerial Competencies and   Academic Year

Impact of the Managerial Competencies on the Grades of the students

To study the impact of the managerial competencies on the grades of the students the descriptive analysis of the managerial competencies with grades were carried out. The summary of descriptive analysis in terms of mean and standard deviation for the core managerial competencies with respect to

78

grades A, B, C and D are shown in Figure 6.7. The grade A denotes a score of 90% and above, B denotes 80% and above C denotes 70%, D denotes 60% and above and F is below 60% and is considered fail.

The A grade students had highest score of 4.3750 for communication competency. For the planning and administration competency the A grade students had a highest score of 3.5188. For the team work competency again, the A grade student had high scores of 3.9250 and multicultural competency attainment was also highest in A grade students with 3.9250. The self management competency for A grade students was also high with an attainment of 4.2313. The students who are good in academic having high grades have high attainment of these managerial competencies. The graphical representation of grades with communication competency, planning and administration, team work, multicultural and self management are shown in Figure 6.8. It is clearly represented graphically in the Communication, Planning and administration, Team work, Multicultural and Self management Competency are high for students with A Grade and low for failures.

The SPSS output for the ANOVA test is shown in Figure 6.9 .for between the groups and within the groups. The value of p are less than 0.05 which means ANOVA results are significant. The students with higher grades (A) have better competencies as compared to those below and the trend continues downwards .

Competencies and Grades		N	Mean	Std. Deviation	Std. Error
Communication	A	24	4.3750	.29996	.06123
	B	41	3.9480	.23022	.03595
	C	21	3.7270	.23843	.05203
	D	11	3.5333	.34383	.10367
	F	5	2.8800	.02981	.01333
	Total	102	3.9059	.43745	.04331
Planning and Administration	A	24	3.5188	.17434	.03559
	B	41	3.2098	.13839	.02161
	C	21	3.0048	.10112	.02207
	D	11	2.8364	.18720	.05644
	F	5	2.4700	.24900	.11136
	Total	102	3.1637	.30662	.03036
Team Work	A	24	3.9250	.31227	.06374
	B	41	3.6390	.16732	.02613
	C	21	3.4794	.14239	.03107
	D	11	3.1394	.28667	.08644
	F	5	3.0133	.07303	.03266
	Total	102	3.5889	.33826	.03349
Multi Cultural	A	24	3.9250	.32471	.06628
	B	41	3.5756	.26812	.04187
	C	21	3.4333	.20083	.04383
	D	11	3.2091	.35342	.10656
	F	5	2.7000	.00000	.00000
	Total	102	3.5461	.39719	.03933
Self Management	A	24	4.2313	.16004	.03267
	B	41	3.8610	.15910	.02485
	C	21	3.5786	.16701	.03644
	D	11	3.2500	.20125	.06068
	F	5	2.9200	.07583	.03391
	Total	102	3.7779	.39026	.03864

Figure 6.7 Descriptive Analysis of the Managerial Competencies with Grades

Figure 6.8 Graphical representation of Communication, Planning and administration , Team work, Multicultural and Self management Competency with Grades

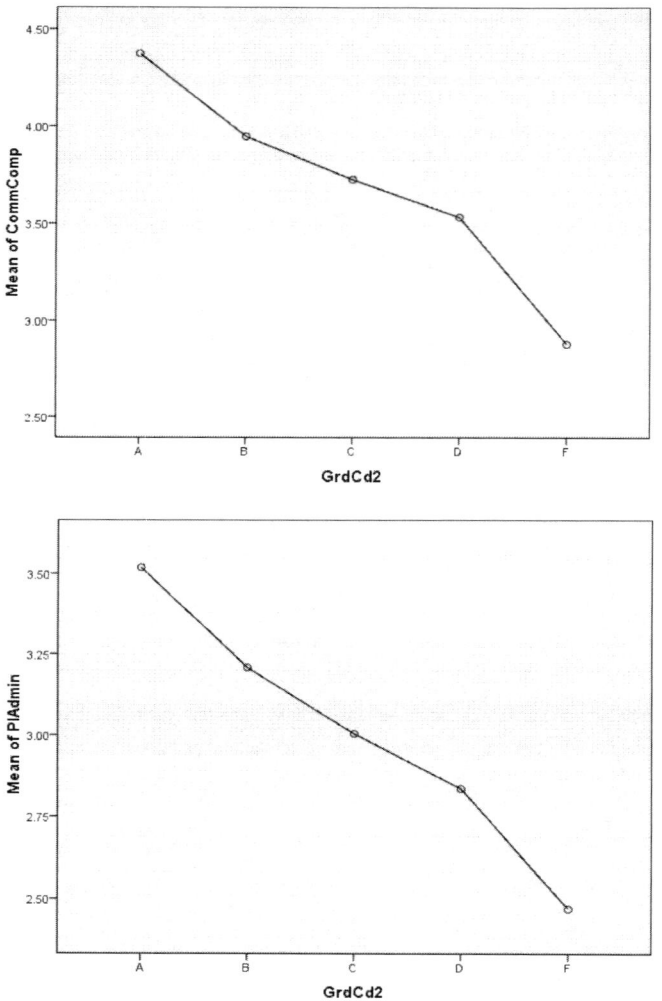

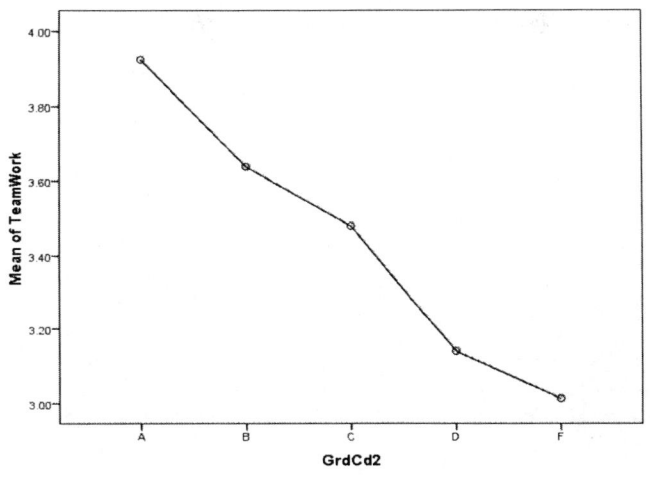

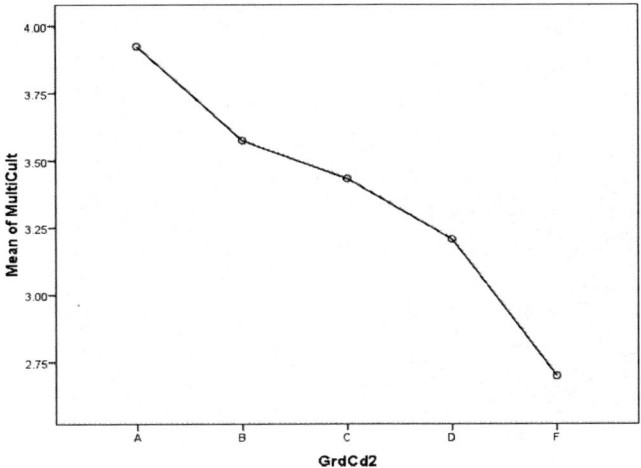

82

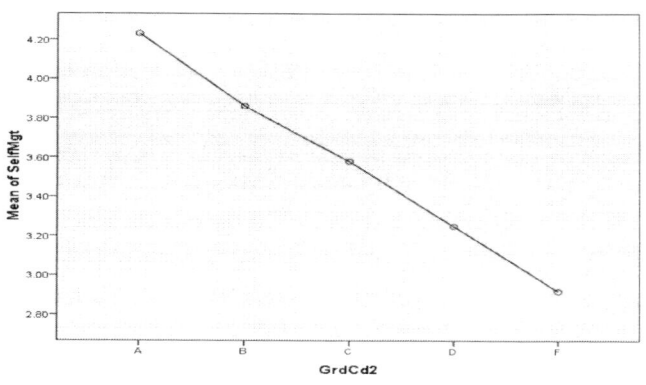

ANOVA		Sum of Squares	df	Mean Square	F	Sig.
Communication	Between Groups	12.815	4	3.204	47.721	.000
	Within Groups	6.512	97	.067		
	Total	19.328	101			
Planning and Administration	Between Groups	7.228	4	1.807	77.275	.000
	Within Groups	2.268	97	.023		
	Total	9.496	101			
Team Work	Between Groups	6.945	4	1.736	36.524	.000
	Within Groups	4.611	97	.048		
	Total	11.556	101			
Multi Cultural	Between Groups	8.577	4	2.144	28.274	.000
	Within Groups	7.356	97	.076		
	Total	15.933	101			
Self Management	Between Groups	12.795	4	3.199	119.919	.000
	Within Groups	2.587	97	.027		
	Total	15.383	101			

Figure 6.9 ANOVA Test for Managerial Competencies and Grades

Correlations Between Managerial Competencies

Mean score analysis of core managerial competencies reveals that a relationship exists between them. Correlation analysis was carried out to statistically test their relationship. This is shown in Figure 6.10. Here Pearson's r is close to 1. This means that there are strong relationships between all variables. Pearson's r is positive (+) this means there positive relationships between all variables. The Sig (2-Tailed) value is 0.000. This means that there are significant positive relationships between variables under study. The value for high correlation range from 5 to 1.0 or -0.5 to -1.0, medium correlation   range from   0.3 to 0.5 or -0.3 to - 0.5 and   low correlation range from 0.1 to .3 or   -0.1 to -0.3. The value of r between communication competency and planning and administration competency is r = .841 and P < 0.001.

.

	Communication	Planning and administration	Team Work	Multicultural
Planning and administration	.841**			
Teamwork	.520**	.659**		
Multicultural	.556**	.587**	.639**	
Self Management	.737**	.820**	.755**	.710**

Figure 6.10 Correlations Between Managerial Competencies
** Correlations significant at the 0.01 level (2-tailed)

The value r for self management competency with others competencies like communication competency   the r = .737 and   P < 0.001 , planning and administration competency the r = .820 and P < 0.001, Team work competency the r = .755 and P < 0.001 and Multicultural competency the r = .710 and P < 0.001.The results shows a significant but high positive correlation exists between communication and planning and administration also of self management with planning and administration, communication, team work and multicultural competencies.

Assessment of the Students Learning Outcomes using Rubric

Rubrics help instructors and students define "quality". From student's perspective, use of rubrics regularly helps to judge their own work, and inculcate a sense of responsibility for the end product. From the instructor's point of view it helps to clarify their expectations, make grading more efficient, convey useful feedback, reduce the time spend in grading students' work ,identifies ways they can improve their work and to grade consistently. They can thus be used to refine teaching skills and assess students learning outcomes. To assess the effectiveness of the competency based learning the rubrics was constructed with 60% weightage given to grades and 40% to self assessments surveys . The score were in scale of 5 and the attainment of 4.7 as shown in Figure 6.11 shows that the students learning outcomes was achieved.

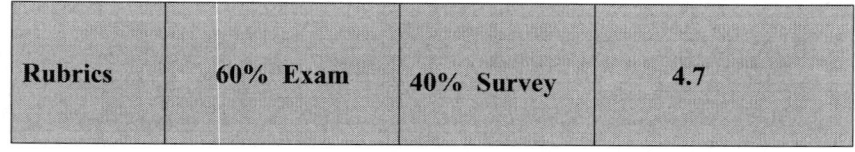

| Rubrics | 60% Exam | 40% Survey | 4.7 |

Figure 6.11 Students Learning Outcomes using Rubric

Chapter 7

CONCLUSION

Global applicants to Business education are increasingly as diverse as the program offerings .Women are making up a progressive record worldwide in terms of admission to Business education. This momentum has also been gaining by leaps and bounds even in the Kingdom of Saudi Arabia. The business education programs have therefore been challenged with the task of developing students with managerial competency for the competitive advantage.

This research was successful in measuring characteristics that are representatives of core dimensions of the five basic managerial competencies (a) Communication Competency, (b) Planning and Administration Competency, (c) Teamwork Competency, (d) Multicultural Competency, (e) Self-Management Competency in university female students of Eastern province of Saudi Arabia. Students benefited by having their managerial competencies defined and develop self awareness by self assessment inventory.

This research proved to be of value addition in Saudi scenario as it will help universities integrate managerial competencies into the program by developmental exercises which will enhance professional development of students and satisfy community needs of advancement. Self-assessment instruments helps to gain insight into the current area of strength and be alerted to areas most needing improvement. The advisory program of college also counsel students in overcoming the areas of weakness.

In light of the domain for research, the study was undertaken to measure the attainment of students learning outcomes. Rubric was used in the study for measuring the achievement of students learning outcome (SLO) using the combination of both direct and indirect assessments. The students learning outcomes scores were high proved in professional development in students. This resulted due to Competency based learning system which were used in introductory management classes to developing managerial competencies among the students by emphasizing on how real world managers uses competencies to address the global challenges.

REFERENCES

AACSB International. (2006). Accreditation. Retrieved from www.aacsb.edu/accreditation, March 7.

Abbey, D. S., Hunt, D. E., & Weiser, J. C. (1985). Variations on a theme by Kolb: A new perspective for understanding counseling and supervision. The Counseling Psychologist, 13, 477-501.

ABDC. (2012) . Austrialian Business dean council ,Future of Management Education Scoping Paper Academy of Management Learning & Education, 2005, Vol. 4, No. 2, 193–212.

ACBSP.(2010).Accreditation Council For Business Schools And Programs.

Allan, P.O.(2010). The history of UK business and management education,Emerald.

Anwar, S. A., Al-Shami, M., & Ahmed, S. A. (2006). Developing a market-oriented MBA program: Practitioners' views from the GCC countries. Journal of International Marketing & Marketing Research, 31(3), 129-139.

Armstrong ,S. (2005). Postgraduate management education in the UK: Lessons from or Lessons for the US Model?. Academy of Management Learning and Education, 4(2): 229-235.

Arnaldo Camuffo, Fabrizio Gerli, Silvia Borgo, Tatiana Somià.(2009). The effects of management education on careers and compensation: A competency-based study of an Italian MBA programme, Journal of Management Development, Vol. 28 Iss: 9, pp.839 – 858.

Asha Alexander and Areej Al Shamrani.(2013). Entrepreneurial Quotient: A Strategic Asset for Personal Branding European Journal of Social Sciences , Volume 38 ,No 2, April,2013.

Asha Alexander, Farah A. Al-Moaibed .(2013) . Measuring Managerial Competencies in Management Program, European Journal of Business and Management , Vol 5, No 11.

Augier, M. and Teece, D.J. (2005). Reflections on (Schumpeterian) leadership: a report on a Seminar on Leadership and Management Education, California Management Review, Vol. 47 No. 2, pp. 114-36.

AWCR. (2013).The Arab World Competitiveness Report 2013. www.weforum.org/reports/arab-world-competitiveness-report-2013.

Barlow, D.H. (1988).Anxiety and Disorders: The Nature and Treatment of Anxiety and Panic,The Guilford Press, New York, NY.

Bell, M. P., Connerley, M. L., & Cocchiara, F. K. (2009). The case for mandatory diversity education. Academy of Management Learning & Education, 8(4), 597-609.

Bennis, W. G., & O'Toole, J. (2005). How business schools lost their way. Harvard business review, 83(5), 96-104.

Borger, Julian (2009) .Saudi Arabia Appoints First Female Minister,The Guardian online". 17 February 2009.

Boyatzis, R. E., Cowen, S. S., & Kolb, D. A. (1995). Innovation in professional education: Steps on a journey from teaching to learning. San Francisco: Jossey-Bass.

Boyatzis, R.E. (1982). The Competent Manager: A Model for Effective Performance, John Wiley & Sons, New York, NY.

Boyatzis, R.E., Stubbs, L. and Taylor, S. (2002).Learning cognitive and emotional intelligence competencies through graduate management education", Academy of Management Journal on Learning and Education, Vol. 1, No. 2, pp. 150-62.

Bray, D.W., Campbell, R.J. and Grant, D.L. (1974). Formative Years in Business: A Long Term AT&T Study of Managerial Lives, John Wiley & Sons, New York, NY.

Buchowicz, B. S., & Buchanan, J. (2008). Level four MBA program design. Journal of Business and BehavioralSciences, 19(2), 58-66.

Campbell, J.P., Dunnette, M.D., Lawler, E.E. III and Weick, K.E. Jr .(1970). Managerial Behavior,Performance, and Effectiveness, McGraw-Hill, New York, NY.

Candace Blayney .(2009) .International Journal Of Management And Marketing Research ,Volume 2 , Number 1 ,2009, Management Competencies:Are They Related To Hotel Performance?

Cherniss, C. and Adler, M. (2000). Promoting Emotional Intelligence in Organizations: MakeTraining in Emotional Intelligence Effective, American Society of Training andDevelopment, Washington, DC.

Connolly, M. (2003). The end of the MBA as we know it?,Academy of Management Learning and Education, Vol. 2 No. 3, pp. 364-6.

Cooper, A. and Graham, D. (2001). Competencies needed to be successful county agents and county supervisors. Journal of Extension [On-line], 39(1). Available at: http://www.joe.org/joe/2001february/rb3.html

Cranton, P. (2006). Understanding and Promoting Transformative Learning: A Guide for Educators of Adults, 2nd Edition. San Francisco: Jossey-Bass.

Darden.(2014).Women in Business and the Role of Business Schools. www..blogs.darden.virginia.edu/deansblog/.../women-in-business-and-the-role

David A Kolb.(1926). Management Learning process, California Management Review, Spring ,1976, Vol XVIII number 3

Dierdorff, E. C., Rubin, R. S., & Morgeson, F. P. (2009). The milieu of management: An integrative framework linking work context to role requirements. Journal of Applied Psychology 2009, Vol. 94, No. 4, 972–988

Dubois, D. D. (1993). Competency-based performance improvement: a strategy for organizational change. Amherst: HRD Press Inc.

Dumas, C., Blodgett, M., Carlson, P., Pant, L., & Venkatraman, M. (2000). Revitalizing the MBA for the new millennium: A collaborative action research approach. International Journal of Value-Based Management, 13(3), 229-253.

Eberhardt, B. J., McGee, P., & Moser, S.(1997).Management concerns regarding MBA education: Effects on recruiting. Journal of Education for Management, 72: 293–296.

Elliott, C. J., & Goodwin, J. S. (1994). MBA programs and business needs: Is there a mismatch? Business Horizons, 37(4), 55.

ESCP. (2013).Europe (SIP) Report 2013/MV: Sharing Information on Progress. www.unprme.org/reports/escpeuropeprmesipreport2013.pdf

Evans, J. M., Treviño, L. K., & Weaver, G. R. (2006). Who's in the ethics driver's seat? Factors influencing ethics in the MBA curriculum. Academy of Management Learning & Education, 5(3), 278-293.

George, D. and Mallery, P. (2003). SPSS for Windows step by step: A simple guide and reference. 11.0 update (4th ed.). Boston: Allyn & Bacon.

Ghoshal, S. (2005). Bad management theories are destroying good management practices. Academy of Management Learning & Education, 4(1): 75–91.

Giacalone, R. A., & Thompson, K. R. (2006). Business ethics and social responsibility education: Shifting the worldview. Academy of Management Learning & Education, 5(3), 266-277.

GMAC .(2013).Profile of GMAT Candidates Executive Summary www.gmac.com/.../GMAT%20Test%20Taker%20Data/2013-gmat-profil.

Goleman, D. (1998). Working with Emotional Intelligence, Bantam Books, New York, NY.

Goleman, D., Boyatzis, R.E. and McKee, A. (2002).Primal Leadership: Realizing the Power of Emotional Intelligence, Harvard Business School Press, Boston, MA.

Greenberg, D. N., Clair, J.A., & MacLean, T. L. (2007). Enacting the Role of Management Professor: Lessons From Athena, Prometheus, and Asclepius. Academy of Management Learning & Education, v. 6, no. 4, pp. 439–457.

Gupta, P., Saunders, P., & Smith, J. (2007). Traditional master of business administration (MBA) versus the MBA with specialization: A disconnection between what business schools offer and what employers seek. The Journal of Education for Business, 82(6), 307-312.

Hellreigel, D., Jackson, S. E., & Slocum, J. W. (2002). Management: A competency-based approach (9th ed.). Cincinnati, OH: Southwestern.

Hellriegel, D., Jackson, S. E., Slocum, J., Staude, G., Amos, T., and Klopper, H. B., Louw, L. & Oosthuizen, T .F. J. (2008). Management. (3rd South African edn.). Cape Town: Oxford.

Howard, A. and Bray, D. (1988). Managerial Lives in Transition: Advancing Age and Changing

Hubble, M.A., Duncan, B.L. and Miller, S.D. (1999).The Heart and Soul of Change: WhatWorks in Therapy, American Psychological Association, Washington, DC.

Human Development Report .(2011).Sustainability and Equity:A Better Future for All, undp.org/en/content/human-development-report-2011

Hunt, D.E. (1987). Beginning with ourselves. Cambridge, MA: Brookline.Introduction to Epistemology. London, UK: SAGE.

Jennifer Lewington .(2013) .The Globe and Mail Is an MBA still worth it http://www.theglobeandmail.com/report-on-business/careers/business-education/is-an-mba-still-worth-it/article15276942/

Johnson, P., & Duberley, J. (2000). Understanding Management Research: An Journal: Journal of Business Research - J BUS RES , vol. 58, no. 4, pp. 467-476, 2005

Kak, Neeraj, Bart Burkhalter, and Merri-Ann Cooper. (2001). Measuring the Competence of Health. Care Providers, Operations Research Issue Paper 2 (1), Published for USAID, Bethesda, Maryland: Quality Assurance Project

Kanfer, F.H. and Goldstein, A.P. (1991).Helping People Change: A Textbook of Methods,4th ed., Allyn & Bacon, Boston, MA.

Khurana, R. (2007). From higher aims to hired hands: The social transformation of American management schools and unfulfilled promise of management as a profession. Princeton, NJ: Princeton University Press.

Kleiman, L. S., & Kass, D. (2007). Giving MBA programs the third degree. Journal of Management Education, 31(1), 81-103.

Kolb, D. A. (1984). Experiential learning: Experience as the source of learning and development. New Jersey: Prentice-Hall

Kolb, A., & Kolb, D. A. (1999). Bibliography of research on experiential learning theory and the Learning Style Inventory. Department of Organizational Behavior, Weatherhead School of Management, Case Western Reserve University,

Kolb, A., & Kolb, D. A. (2005). Learning Styles and Learning Spaces: Enhancing Experiential Learning in Higher Education Academy of Management Learning & Education, 2005, Vol. 4, No. 2, 193–212.

Kolb, D. A. (1999)a. Learning Style Inventory, Version 3. TRG

Kolb, D. A. (1999)b. Learning Style Inventory-Version 3: Technical specifications. TRG Hay/McBer, Training Resources Group.

Kotter, J.P. (1982). The General Managers, Free Press, New York, NY.

Lengnick-Hall, C. A., & Sanders, M. M. (1997). Designing effective learning systems for management education: Student roles, requisite variety, and practicing what we teach. Academy of Management Journal, 40(6), 1334-1368.

Lewis, L. H., & Williams, C. J. (1994). Experiential learning: Past and present. In L. Jackson & R. S. Caffarella(Eds.), Experiential learning: A new approach (pp. 5-16). San Francisco: Jossey-Bass.

Liu Yah Olan ,Bhawana Sainger ,Ilham Sentosa ,Chee Wei Ming.(2012). An Empirical Testing of Managerial Competencies of Industrial Managers in Sichuan Province of China, International Journal of Independent Research and Studies Vol. 1, No.1; Jan 2012.

Luthans, F., Hodgetts, R.M. and Rosenkrantz, S.A. (1988). Real Managers, Ballinger Press, Cambridge, MA

Margaret M. Hopkins, Diana Bilimoria, (2008). Social and emotional competencies predicting success for male and female executives, Journal of Management Development, Vol. 27 Iss: 1, pp.13– 35.

McClelland, D.C. (1973). Testing for competence rather than intelligence , American Psychologist, Vol. 28 No. 1, pp. 1-40.

Meenakshi Radhakrishnan-Swami.(2007).What They Don't Teach You at B-schoolTata McGraw-Hill Education.

Mintzberg, H. (2004). Managers not MBAs, A hard look at the soft practice of managing and management development. London: Prentice Hall

MOHE.(2010). Ministry of Higher education,Deputyship for planning and education , General Department for Planning and Stasticss,Women in Higher Education , Saudi Initiatives and aheivement.

Morrow, C.C., Jarrett, M.Q. and Rupinski, M.T. (1997), An investigation of the effect and economic utility of corporate-wide training, Personnel Psychology, Vol. 50, pp. 91-119.

Navarro, P. (2008). The MBA core curricula of top-ranked U.S. business schools: A study in failure? Academy of Management Learning & Education, 7(1), 108-123.

Neda Tiraieyari, Khairuddin Idris, Jegak Uli and Azimi Hamzah.(2010). Competencies Influencing Extension Workers' Job Performance in Relation to the Good Agricultural Practices in Malaysia. American Journal of Applied Sciences 7 (10): 1379-1386.

Pascarella, E.T. and Terenzini, P.T. (1991), How College Affects Students: Findings and Insights from Twenty Years of Research, Jossey-Bass, San Francisco, CA.

Peter,K.(2006).MBA Challenge - Ashridge,2006 https://www.ashridge.org.uk/Media-Library/.../MBAChallenge.pdf

Pfeffer, J., & Fong, C. (2002). The end of business schools? Less success than meets the eye. Academy of ManagementLearning and Education, 1(1), 78-95.

Pfeffer, J., & Fong, C. T. (2003). Assessing business schools: Reply to Connolly. Academy of Management Learning & Education, 2, 368-370. doi:10.5465/AMLE.2003.11901962

Pfeffer, J., & Fong, C. T. (2004). The business school "business": Some lessons from the U.S. experience. Journal of Management Studies, 41, 1501-1520. doi:10.1111/j.1467-6486.2004.00484.x

Podolny, J. M. (2009). The buck stops (and starts) at business school. Harvard business review, 87(6), 62-67.

Richard E. Boyatzis, (2006) .An overview of intentional change from a complexity perspective, Journal of Management Development, Vol. 25 Iss: 7, pp.607 - 623

Rubin Pillar.(2008).Managerial competencies of hospital managers in South Africa: a survey of managers in the public and private sectors Human Resources for Health, 6:4 http://www.human-resources-health.com/content/6/1/4

Rubin, R. S., & Dierdorff, E. C. (2009). How relevant Is the MBA? Assessing the alignment of required curricula and required managerial competencies. Academy of Management Learning & Education, 8(2), 208-224

Rynes, S. L., & Trank, C. Q. (1999). Behavioral science in the business school curriculum: Teaching in a changing institutional environment. Academy of Management Review, 24: 808–824.

Rynes, S. L., Trank, C. Q., Lawson, A. M., & Ilies, R. (2003). Behavioral coursework in management education: Growing evidence of a legitimacy crisis. Academy of Management Learning & Education, 2: 269–283.

SIDF.(2013). Future Challenges facing Saudi Industries , Saudi Industrial Developmental Fund ,www.sidf.gov.sa

Spencer, L.M. Jr and Spencer, S.M..(1993). Competence at Work: Models for Superior Performance, John Wiley & Sons, New York, NY.

Spitzberg, B. H., & Cupach, W. R. (1984). Interpersonal Communication Competence. Beverly Hills, CA: Sage. 43, pp. 259-86.

Suskie, L. (2004). Assessing Student Learning: A common sense guide. Anker Publishing Company: Bolton, Ma.

Swanson, D. L. (2004). The buck stops here: Why universities must reclaim business ethics education. Journal of Academic Ethics, 2(1), 43-61

Tannenbaum, S. I. (1997). Enhancing continuous learning: Diagnostic findings from multiple companies. Human Resource Management, 36: 437–452.Times, Guilford Press, New York, NY.

USSABC.(2009).The U.S.-Saudi Arabian Business Council, The Education Sector in the Kingdom of Saudi Arabia

Villardi, B. Q. and Vergara, S.C .(2013).How Do Business School Professors Learn To Teach Management Students? Learning And Pedagogical Assumptions Guiding Practice Olkc, 2013 Theme: Translation, Transition & Transmission.

Widget Finn. (2012).MBA women: breaking down barriers at business schoolhttp://www.telegraph.co.uk/education/educationadvice/9683856/MBA-women-breaking-down-barriers-at-business-school.html

Winter, D.G., McClelland, D.C. and Stewart, A.J. (1981). A New Case for the Liberal Arts:Assessing Institutional Goals and Student Development, Jossey-Bass, San Francisco, CA.

Wittaya Chansiri and Boonchom Srisa-ard .(2009). Core Competency of Public Universities Supporting-Line Administrators in Thailand. The Social Sciences, 4: 128-132.

World Bank .(2007). The Status of Progress of Women in the Middle East and North Africa, Washington D.C, 2007.

WEF.(2014).World Economic Forum, Global Competitiveness Report 2014-2015 - Reports - World www.weforum.org/global...2014.../box-the-need-for-structural-reform.

Druck: KN Digital Printforce GmbH · Schockenriedstraße 37 · 70565 Stuttgart